W9-AEW-713

A manual for students, teachers,
professionals, and clients

This book is dedicated to Two Twelve Associates,
the extraordinary design firm that has been my
home and inspiration for almost three decades.

THE WAYFINDING HANDBOOK

Information Design for Public Places

WITHDRAWN

DAVID GIBSON

Foreword by Christopher Pullman

Princeton Architectural Press
New York

Published by Princeton Architectural Press
37 East Seventh Street
New York, New York 10003

For a free catalog of books, call 1.800.722.6657.
Visit our website at www.papress.com.

Series Editor: Ellen Lupton
Project Editor: Linda Lee
Acquisitions Editor: Clare Jacobson
Consulting Editor: Juanita Dugdale
Designers: Laura Varacchi, Vijay Mathews, and Julie Park
of Two Twelve Associates

Special thanks to: Nettie Aljian, Sara Bader, Dorothy Ball,
Nicola Bednarek, Janet Behning, Becca Casbon, Carina Cha,
Penny (Yuen Pik) Chu, Russell Fernandez, Pete Fitzpatrick,
Wendy Fuller, Jan Haux, Aileen Kwun, Nancy Eklund Later,
Aaron Lim, Laurie Manfra, Katharine Myers, Ceara O'Leary,
Lauren Nelson Packard, Jennifer Thompson, Arnoud
Verhaeghe, Paul Wagner, Joseph Weston, and Deb Wood
of Princeton Architectural Press—Kevin C. Lippert, publisher

Library of Congress Cataloging-in-Publication Data

Gibson, David, 1950–
 The wayfinding handbook : information design for public places /
David Gibson ; foreword by Christopher Pullman.
   p. cm. — (Design briefs)
 Includes bibliographical references and index.
 ISBN 978-1-56898-769-9 (pbk. : alk. paper)
 1. Signs and signboards—Design. 2. Public spaces—Psychological
aspects. 3. Communication in architectural design. I. Title.

 NC1002.S54G53 2009
 741.6—DC22

                                              2008025826

FOREWORD

Exiting the subway in the middle of a city or stepping off the elevator onto a strange floor is momentarily disorientating: you scan the space to figure out where you are and find clues that will lead you where you want to go. This scanning is similar to searching for an article in a magazine or perusing the home page of a website to figure out how it is organized and how to reach a specific section.

All these reflex actions are about wayfinding.

This book demystifies the fascinating process of providing the necessary clues and environmental information that help people orient themselves and intuitively find their way. I first met the author, David Gibson, when he was a graduate student in the Yale graphic design program. As David's career developed, he made wayfinding a specialty of his design practice. He learned to think through the underlying mental puzzle of orientation, codify the steps to planning and implementing a design solution, and navigate the public process of initiating and successfully concluding a project. For anyone curious about this line of work, *The Wayfinding Handbook* is a good place to start.

Wayfinding, of course, has been around ever since the first bunch of cave men got lost trying to find their way home from a wooly mammoth hunt, but it only became a profession in the twentieth century.

A specialized subset of environmental graphic design, wayfinding matured concurrently with the rise of the internet's soup of too much information with too little context, where clear orientation signals have become essential.

The principles of wayfinding, while most often applied to spaces, also pertain to other situations. Psychologist and industrial designer Donald Norman's book *The Design of Everyday Things* (1988) raised public attention (and ire) about inadequately designed products: appliances that are impossible to figure out, light switches placed where you least expect them, or doors oriented without regard for the direction they swing. That the operation of products and spaces should be self-evident, humane, and intuitive may seem obvious, he argues, but it is often not the case.

Norman's common sense about design proved to be a bellwether of a new era of consumer advocacy and sophisticated product testing. Although the concept has been an intrinsic part of the design process for ages, the term *user interface design* has come into common use relatively recently. The idea that the designer should be the advocate of the end user took hold in the 1990s in both product design and website development. Industrial-design firms and internet studios began employing psychologists, anthropologists, and ethnographers—all professionals trained to understand human behavior—to help designers predict how a given form would be under-stood and used. User testing and rapid prototyping (make something quickly, give it to the target users, watch to see what they make of it, revise, and repeat) became typical practice.

It is easy to assume that because the placement or content of a sign is obvious to the designer—or the button on a computer screen looks like that or should be here—that the end user will find it obvious too. But I have watched as test subjects fumble through a home page everybody on the design team thinks is airtight, unable to locate the target content or misunderstanding the behavior of a button. It is all about users under-standing where they are and what they need to do.

I think my early interest in wayfinding developed because my father was in the map business. The house was always littered with maps showing various parts of the world. I loved to look at them because they encap-sulated so much information that made it possible to imagine the feeling, the terrain, and the look of some distant place. (Ironically, when I got married I discovered my in-laws never used maps. They basically wouldn't go anywhere they couldn't get to with verbal directions—a weird precursor to today's in-dash GPS voice navigation gadgets.) Later, as a canoe guide in Canada, I relied on maps to navigate from lake to lake, on signal trees to mark a portage, and on blazes to follow the trail.

My own career has always reflected this spatial awareness. As an undergraduate I took pre-architecture courses and became sensitive to how buildings and other structures can—or unfortunately, in many cases, do not—provide signals that aid orientation. In graphic design graduate school, I became fascinated with how in a book or multipage communication subtle grids and other underlying structures support the content. In way-finding, these structures provide a predictable location for different kinds of information and hierarchical clues that improve both comprehension (this is the title, byline, or footnote) and navigation (here is the page number; now you're in a new section).

During a stint as graphics coordinator in the office of architect and designer George Nelson in New York, I deployed these strategies in exhibition design, and later in my first real wayfinding project: signage for the huge Lincoln Hospital in the Bronx. Guiding patients with a limited understanding of English through a warren of uncoordinated multifloor spaces confronted me with the tricky problem of providing legible, economical, and easy-to-maintain signs at every conceivable decision point in this maze.

Then in 1973 when I joined WGBH, the public broad-casting station in Boston, I began to understand how ideas of orientation applied to time-based media. Video has its own set of conventions that orient the viewer to physical space (point of view), visual and aural focus (what we see and hear), and time. Interactive media have yet other special conventions, but many of the principles are the same.

Only recently, however, have I become really immersed in architectural wayfinding. That came about because WGBH had to move from its home of forty years and build a whole new headquarters; as vice president of design, I was asked to be on the management team. This also included the president, the treasurer (responsible for the fiscal management of the project), and the construction manager (responsible for managing relationships with the general contractor and all the subspecialties). My role was to help define the character of the new facility (its formal appearance, cultural feel, and functional needs), select the architect, serve as design client, and oversee the informational and wayfinding graphic program for the project.

This five-year effort made me fully appreciate the essential nature of the processes outlined in this book. The architects were, of course, critical in supplying the building with a form that expresses its basic organization and the logic of its circulation. We consulted with specialists who understood the technical code requirements of public signing and had the depth of experience to propose systems both economical and easy to update, and we worked with our own staff to define the character of the graphics and test the logic of our decisions.

The process resulted in a facility that works very well for us, but had I been able to read this book first, I would have been better prepared, both as a designer and as a client. Because you are reading it right now, you are already a step ahead! And soon you will have a more holistic view about how to help people understand and enjoy the spaces they visit.

Christopher Pullman

Christopher Pullman is a design consultant and senior critic at Yale University School of Art. An AIGA fellow and medalist, he is the former vice president of Branding and Visual Communications at WGBH Boston, where he managed design from 1973 to 2008.

PREFACE

The Wayfinding Handbook is intended to be a user's guide to the art and science of the specialized design discipline that has occupied me for the better part of the past thirty years. This book is a record of what I have learned about wayfinding design, the summation of many rich experiences I have had as a principal of Two Twelve Associates working for all kinds of clients across the country. In undertaking these projects, I've been inspired and educated not only by the people I work for but also by fellow designers and colleagues who work alongside me.

This creative design work has been a joyful endeavor and reflects my generally optimistic view of the world. As a baby boomer who came of age in Canada in the 1960s and '70s, I have always believed that we should work together to make a better world, that the common good is more important than individual experience. The wayfinding designer's work lies at the intersection of people and places. It is a collective enterprise, done with and for people, seeking to make extraordinary, interesting, and accessible places. This discipline is intellectually engaging because it allows one to learn about fascinating institutions, meet interesting people, and use design to transform public spaces. In comparison, other types of design problems seem rather narrowly focused. The wayfinding projects described here are often complex and influential because they affect large populations.

In undertaking this book, I wanted to create a handy guide to the discipline that will serve as a textbook for design professors and students; a design resource for recent graduates and mature designers interested in wayfinding; and a source of ideas and inspiration for practicing professionals, managers, and owners. The book explains what wayfinding is, where it came from, who needs it, and how projects unfold. This primer delivers a concise overview of our process, from planning and strategy through typography, color, and three-dimensional design to practical considerations that help designers successfully complete a project. The photographs/images featured in this book include documentation of Two Twelve's work as well as contributions from respected designers, industry leaders, and signage enthusiasts.

I hope you'll learn something and be inspired— and that the handbook will become battered and well-handled in the process.

David Gibson

1 THE DISCIPLINE

1.1 PEOPLE AND PLACES

Order is no guarantee of understanding. Sometimes just the opposite is true...
Cities don't come in chapters with restaurants in one section and museums
in another; their order is organic, sometimes confusing, never alphabetic.
To really experience a city fully, you have to acknowledge confusion.
RICHARD SAUL WURMAN, *INFORMATION ANXIETY*

The heart of a civilization throbs wherever people come
together to work, play, shop, study, perform, worship, or
just interact. Crowded into bustling spaces, they share
the richness and diversity of human experience as well as
its challenges. In these spaces people may "find their way"
in the existential sense, but they also become overwhelmed
or disoriented if they physically lose their way. Wayfinding
design provides guidance and the means to help people feel
at ease in their surroundings.

LEARN ABOUT
The emergence of the
wayfinding discipline

People throughout history have gravitated to town centers, market squares, and vibrant public spaces filled with global wares, such as New York City's Rockefeller Center, Galleria Vittorio Emanuele in Milan, or the Grand Bazaar in Istanbul. Houses of worship once set apart from the fray, where people sought sanctuary, now often sit side by side with busy commercial centers, libraries, schools, restaurants, residential complexes, and cultural spaces. Any lively neighborhood is appealing, whether its evolution was organic, like Greenwich Village in New York, the hutongs of Beijing, the medinas in Fez, or planned in the spirit of new urbanism, like Disney's Celebration community in Florida. The real fabric of human existence is woven together in settings where people go about their daily routine. As the iconoclastic writer Bernard Rudofsky points out in *Streets for People* (1969): "Altogether, cities correspond closely to the ideas and ideals of their inhabitants. They are the tangible expression of a nation's spirit, or lack of spirit."[1]

Over time cities, spaces, complexes, and buildings fill up with information, markers, and symbols. Sometimes charming results emerge, as depicted in popular books on vernacular, "undesigned" signs, but the effect can also be ugly or chaotic, or both. The wayfinding designer is responsible for enhancing how a space— whether public, commercial, or private—is experienced by finding order in chaos without destroying character. People will always need to know how to reach their destination, where they are, what is happening there, and how to exit. Great wayfinding systems employ explicit signs and information as well as implicit symbols and landmarks that together communicate with accuracy and immediacy. This handbook explores the purpose and scope of wayfinding systems for spaces where people convene and how they are planned, designed, and produced.

THE ORIGIN OF WAYFINDING

Many wayfinding designers are baby boomers whose political and environmental consciousness was informed by the futile Vietnam conflict and subsequent social ferment of the 1970s. Motivated by a sense of public communal mission and zeal for creative experimentation, they gradually moved the wayfinding field into the twenty-first century, building upon the foundation of experience established by earlier design pioneers over the course of the previous century. War—World War II, that is—had an inadvertently positive impact on their careers as well, either by forcing talented Europeans, such as Alvin Lustig, to emigrate to North America where opportunity awaited or by providing art and design training to many a veteran, including John Follis of Pasadena, California.

During the 1960s Cold War period, critics, scholars, and designers felt an urgent need to humanize increasingly complex modern urban spaces. The design discipline that evolved in response has been called architectural graphics, signage or sign-system design, environmental graphic design, and wayfinding. Over

time, enterprising firms and individuals, such as Lance Wyman, who won early acclaim for his Mexico '68 Olympics symbols, began to specialize in sign system design. Some firms offered wayfinding design in tandem with other services, including exhibition, product, interior, and corporate-identity design, the latter the precursor of branding services.

The long and notable list of principals of pioneering American firms includes Ivan Chermayeff, Tom Geismar, Rudolph de Harak, and Lella and Massimo Vignelli. Their contemporaries in the United Kingdom included founding partners of Pentagram, now a global collaborative, as well as the venerable designer F. H. K. Henrion. Wayfinding design has always attracted women, particularly in the early years when the field offered a much better platform for career advancement and business ownership than more established disciplines such as architecture. For example, Barbara Stauffacher Solomon and Deborah Sussman (a protégée of Ray and Charles Eames) flourished in California, while Elaine Lustig Cohen and Jane Davis Doggett made early inroads on the East Coast and were later followed by Sue Gould and Ann Dudrow.

Three writers are largely responsible for popularizing the term *wayfinding*, which seems to have stuck as the best name to describe both the process and profession dedicated to helping people navigate. In 1960, urban planner and teacher Kevin Lynch coined the term in his landmark book about urban spaces, *The Image of the City*. Lynch explains that "way-finding" relates to the process of forming a mental picture of one's surroundings based on sensation and memory.

"To become completely lost is perhaps a rather rare experience for most people in the modern city. We are supported by the presence of others and by special way-finding devices: maps, street numbers, route signs, bus placards. But let the mishap of disorientation once occur, and the sense of anxiety and even terror that accompanies it reveals to us how closely it is linked to our sense of balance and well-being."[2]

Twenty years later Romedi Passini wrote *Wayfinding in Architecture* and probed the subject in greater depth. In 1992 he coauthored *Wayfinding: People, Signs, and Architecture* with Paul Arthur, a Canadian professor-cum-designer who made a personal mission of advancing the field by reigniting interest in Lynch's observations. In addition to coining the term *signage*, Arthur also developed innovative wayfinding projects and eventually became a fellow of the Society for Environmental Graphic Design (SEGD), the international association dedicated to advancing the field. Originally founded by a handful of designers who wished to share their expertise in different fields, SEGD today serves many professionals from architecture, planning, graphic design, exhibition design, product design, and interior design who practice wayfinding. Over time, *environmental graphic design* became the preferred umbrella term to describe any communications intended for spatial application,

ranging from wayfinding sign programs to branded spaces, exhibitions, and even public art. SEGD's annual competitions, website, and publications provide a lively forum for new work to be shared and discussed by the global community of practitioners. Most successful wayfinding designers start with a solid design education that leads to an entry-level position in a major firm, and soon join SEGD to stay abreast of professional and technical developments.

THE AGE OF INFORMATION ARCHITECTURE

In 1976 architect Richard Saul Wurman chose "The Architecture of Information" as the theme for an annual convention of the American Institute of Architects, setting the precedent for a book he produced two decades later entitled *Information Architects* (1996). Individually, the projects discussed in the book are conventional communication vehicles—maps, diagrams, books, sign systems, symbols, and websites— but presented as a collection, they represent a design specialization that had been maturing for much of the twentieth century without a name until Wurman coined *information architecture.*

In one of his most popular books, *Information Anxiety* (1989), Wurman warned of the emotionally disturbing effects of information overload at a time when people were captivated by the novelty of personal computing technologies. With twenty years'

hindsight, this realization seems obvious, but at the time the assertion that more information does not equal better understanding had a major impact on designers and the general public.

Wurman's ideas; brilliant books by author-publisher Edward Tufte about the visualization of data, notably his much-heralded *Visual Display of Quantitative Information* (1983); and the growing demand for good information design in the public realm have all had a positive trickle-down effect on wayfinding. Greater emphasis on the need for experienced information designers has in turn validated the profession of the practitioners, who often work in anonymity. Tufte's books, for instance, consistently receive enthusiastic endorsements from mainstream press such as the *New York Times* and *Scientific American*. While his works are carefully researched and beautifully crafted, they are not just visually appealing but also satisfy an apparent public appetite for arcane content expressed diagrammatically. One of his most popular examples turns a map of the Napoleonic army's doomed march to and from Russia into a dramatic graph depicting the radical reduction in troops due to illness and death, all cleverly revealed in a simple, extraordinary chart.

Map design is an important subset of wayfinding with its own fascinating history. Existing since the dawn of language, maps represent a chronology of all kinds of human pursuits, whether cultural, intellectual, economic, or political. The most iconic examples of

wayfinding maps were designed to help the public navigate early transportation systems such as railway networks and subways. Though global positioning and other digital technologies have moved spatial diagrams off sign panels and into cars or handheld devices, mapping remains at the forefront of the field today.

Symbol design is equally important to wayfinding. Symbols provide a shortcut way for large groups of people who may not share a common language to communicate. Authorities who manage transportation facilities and other public places are indebted to Tom Geismar. The landmark symbol-sign study project he directed for the American Institute of Graphic Arts, started in the 1970s, organized a coherent family of fifty symbols that today serves as a foundation for many symbol sets developed for use in parks and other venues (see chapter 3.4).

TODAY AND TOMORROW

Wayfinding design has finally come of age and not a moment too soon. As predicted by many a twentieth-century prophet, our cities continue to sprawl as their infrastructures grow unwiedly. Getting people from place to place and orienting them in complex spaces is increasingly complicated, especially with all the transportation options now available—from highway to Segway. The expanding complexity of the world's built environment seems to be growing in direct pro-portion to the demise of the natural one.

Sophisticated international communications, fueled by the internet explosion, have accelerated concern about the pace of global change and inspired the newest generation of designers to mobilize for action like never before. These young professionals face an exciting era of technological invention, social upheaval, and radical creativity. The beginning of the twenty-first century may, in fact, become wayfinding's renaissance, with a number of capable firms springing up each year and more than enough work to go around to sustain them.

There is no question, however, that the wayfinding field is very competitive, which puts pressure on firms to produce outstanding work and stay current with technological developments. Designers who once sealed deals with a handshake must now follow bureaucratic procedures to secure a client contract, and principals must negotiate good employee compensation packages to attract and keep talented staff on board. These trends demonstrate the health of the profession: wayfinding remains an open-ended field with a promising future for young practitioners who think spatially, love to travel, and have a knack for communicating. For the wayfinding profession to remain healthy and prosper, students need to recognize the fascinating, multidisciplinary opportunities it offers.

1 Bernard Rudofsky, *Streets for People: A Primer for Americans* (Garden City, NY: Doubleday, 1969), 17.
2 Kevin Lynch, *The Image of the City* (Cambridge, MA: MIT Press, 1960), 4.

1.2 THE SPECTRUM OF PROJECTS

We believe that the designer should be able to design anything,
"from spoon to the city" because the basic discipline of design is one,
the only things that change are the specifics.
LELLA AND MASSIMO VIGNELLI, *DESIGN–VIGNELLI*

During the past forty years, as the environmental graphic design profession matured, the range of wayfinding projects rapidly expanded. In the 1970s the early professional practice of architectural graphics mainly entailed designing signs for architects' and developers' buildings. Today almost every type of public space and most private complexes require a wayfinding scheme. The clients who commission signage systems for these venues—together with the designers and fabricators who create them—belong to a dynamic, creative industry.

? LEARN ABOUT
Different types of clients who hire wayfinding designers and the kinds of projects they commission

WAYFINDING MARKETS AND PROJECT TYPES

Visual surveys on the following two spreads give an overview of the diversity of client and project types. *Who Hires a Wayfinding Designer?* on pages 20–21 presents the different industries and market sectors that require wayfinding systems. On one hand are large centers for transportation, education, and healthcare, where effective and efficient signage is crucial; on the other are sports arenas, hotels, and mixed-use developments, where good wayfinding can support a rich customer experience. In urban areas wayfinding systems become a part of the civic infrastructure and the public narrative of the city.

Within various business sectors there are many different kinds of projects. *What Do Wayfinding Clients Need?* on pages 22–23 provides a typology. These can vary from a signage system for an individual building, or for a whole campus or building complex. These two visual surveys offer a framework for understanding the scope of wayfinding design.

WHY PEOPLE NEED WAYFINDING SYSTEMS

Successful wayfinding design depends on understanding three variables: the nature of the client organization, the people with whom the organization communicates, and the type of environment in which the system will be installed. It is important to research and define all three of these variables clearly at the outset of a project. In developing the wayfinding strategy and designing the sign system, the designer will have to create a family of sign types that not only addresses primary information and wayfinding needs but also recognizes secondary issues and audiences with an appropriate information hierarchy and sign-messaging protocols.

The wayfinding requirements of a municipal client must often address different user groups in various settings. The institution interacts with a diverse community—locals and tourists—all coming to visit city centers, city parks, or other public spaces. In addition, the environmental graphics need to attract commercial developers in urban-development opportunities.

A corporate client, for example, may need to complete interior signage for a new office building to obtain a legal certificate of occupancy and set up the building for tenants. That same corporation may also wish to use branded signage to advertise and attract customers, or to signal a change of corporate ownership by rebranding signage at multiple branch locations (see chapter 3.1).

Other private institutions have their own particular signage specifications. In the case of a hospital, for instance, the facilities department may issue a Request for Proposal (RFP) for wayfinding signage to connect a new building to a larger campus. In their view the primary audience for the signage consists of the patients and visitors who need to find physicians, treatment centers, and other destinations quickly. Secondary audiences include internal groups like doctors, nursing staff, and maintenance and service people.

As in most multidepartmental organizations, the hospital sign system affects many departments and personnel. For example, the development office may be obligated to name the new building after a major donor. The architect of the new building will be concerned that signage is integrated effectively with the architectural design intent. The communications department may decide to use the opportunity to roll out a new institutional identity. Operators of the hospital cafeteria or gift shop may have requirements or even lease agreements that need to be considered regarding the scope of their signage. An effective wayfinding program can easily balance the needs of the different constituencies, supporting and enabling a positive experience.

WHO IS THE CLIENT?

The client is either an individual or a large team of people that provides direction and supervision and sets project parameters. A typical client could be the owner of a single property or developer of a large complex, the operator of a transit line, or a facility manager of a hospital. Clients often act on their own behalf but can also enlist people, such as a project-management consultant or company, to represent them at various

The Design Principal

Our company, Two Twelve Associates, has always been dedicated to creating designs and public information systems that improve the dynamics between people and the places they visit. As Two Twelve evolved from a small studio to a planning consultancy, it soon won bigger contracts that demanded a higher level of supervisory responsibility. The core lesson we've learned over time is that designing a great product goes hand in hand with delivering value for the money.

Whether your client for a wayfinding project is a corporation or an institution, this means paying attention to the bottom line: understanding the budget and managing it all the way through the project, letting the client know when requests for changes will push fees over estimate and offering solutions to cut production costs or streamline the work process. Beyond meeting these basic expectations, designers should look for unique ways to add value to the project or product. You need to understand your client's business objectives, both explicit and inherent, and ensure that your design solutions meet them.

A developer of a new building, for example, seeks the highest rents possible, so the designer needs to figure out where value can be built into every aspect of the solution. Is it emphasizing a desirable address with a striking identification sign? Highlighting world-class architecture with special details? Or maybe it's just helping to get the building to market faster by getting the code-required signage installed within two months.

Other kinds of projects have other objectives. The builder of a stadium delivers value by giving home-team fans a good wayfinding experience via festive, team-branded signage that adds to the excitement of game day and makes it easy to get from street to seat and back again. This is a form of brand extension that gives the fans subtle incentive to come back, game after game, season after season. Loyal fans, in turn, add value to the home-team franchise, and that value enables the stadium owner to charge a premium for sponsors and concessionaires to promote their brands and products within the stadium environment.

Project objectives can be that simple, and that complex. The designer's job is to do the necessary homework: researching and understanding the client's business goals well enough to add significant value through the signage and wayfinding program.

Ann Harakawa, principal of Two Twelve Associates and a Yale University graduate, has over twenty-five years' experience working in the design industry.

stages in the process. Many wayfinding projects are managed by architects who represent the interests of their clients and also strive to ensure the holistic interpretation of their design vision for the building or complex. Often, a construction manager may be hired to supervise the fabrication and installation of wayfinding elements along with the rest of the architecture.

Who Hires a Wayfinding Designer?

These images illustrate the diversity of clients who need wayfinding systems and the kinds of facilities they operate. Even though every space is unique, venues in each category share typical wayfinding challenges.

EDUCATION AND CULTURE
Colleges and universities, museums, cultural centers, visitor centers, zoos, and aquariums

HOSPITALITY
Hotels and resorts, planned communities, convention centers

SPORTS AND ENTERTAINMENT
Arenas and stadiums, sports complexes, theme parks, performance spaces

COMMERCIAL REAL ESTATE
Buildings, mixed-use developments with residential, hospitality, and retail spaces

CORPORATIONS

Private office interiors, corporate campuses, building complexes, branch or franchise location

RETAIL

Individual stores, department stores, shopping centers

HEALTH CARE

Hospitals, hospital complexes, research campuses

GOVERNMENT

Municipal centers, state and federal complexes, urban spaces and plazas, streetscapes, downtowns, public parks, playgrounds

TRANSPORTATION

Airports; public transportation: subway, bus, commuter rail, intercity trains, ferry services; ship terminals and ports

21

What Do Wayfinding Clients Need?

These images illustrate the range of design projects. The complexity of the assignment grows in direct proportion to the scale and challenges of the client's property. Developing a signage program for a single building can take a few months; a rail system might take years.

INDIVIDUAL SIGN
A single landmark or feature sign

SYSTEM SIGNAGE
Signage for multiple locations, branches, or franchises operated by one owner or manager, ranging from park systems to consumer banks

WAYFINDING FOR BUILDING COMPLEXES
Exterior and interior signage for a group of buildings, public or private

CAMPUS WAYFINDING
Wayfinding system for a group of buildings operating together on one site, often institutional

NETWORK SIGNAGE
Wayfinding design for multiple stops along a route including bus, rail, or subway lines, and highways

OPEN SPACE SIGNAGE
Exterior signage for individual parks, streets, or plazas; for trails and greenways; and for urban downtowns

BUILDING SIGNAGE
Signage for an individual structure, exterior and/or interior

1.3 THE WAYFINDING DESIGNER

To communicate is to be alive, to be active, in relation with others…For communication is essentially an interchange, a question and a reply, an action and a reaction between an individual and the environment in which he lives.
MAURICE FABRE, *A HISTORY OF COMMUNICATIONS*

Before we dive into the specifics of planning and design, it is useful to step back and ask: Who designs the projects described in the previous section? How does someone become a successful wayfinding designer? How are they trained, and where do they work? It helps to understand that wayfinding is a subset of environmental graphic design, a larger discipline that embraces many specializations including architecture and the design of graphic communications, maps, exhibitions, products, and interiors. Another way to understand the profession is by analyzing project structures and how designers fit into them. The charts in this chapter of small, medium, and large projects show different combinations of players.

LEARN ABOUT
Environmental graphic design as a career path and how designers work in teams

BECOMING A WAYFINDING DESIGNER

In general there is no single, obvious career path for becoming a wayfinding or environmental graphic designer, but rather an indirect journey that combines interests, talents, obsessions, ideas, training, experience, and mentorship. Just as the profession is eclectic, so are the backgrounds of the people who are considered the master practitioners today; it follows that an ideal model for an environmental graphic design education does not yet exist.

Before environmental graphic design became a recognized profession, designers from a variety of disciplines identified the demand for architectural signage and wayfinding systems. They began to offer these design services as specializations within a more general practice, usually architecture, interiors, communications design, or product design. It took years before academic courses on signage and wayfinding design became common, although more schools and universities commit to establishing them every year (see Other Voices page 29).

What has gradually evolved in lieu of organized curricula is an ad hoc apprenticeship system, where young designers with suitable skill sets become protégés of an established wayfinding designer or design team. Alternatively, established designers sometimes embrace environmental graphic design later in their careers. For instance, Paula Scher, principal of Pentagram, is a gifted typographer who started out designing record jackets and now creates idiosyncratic type compositions in, on, and around buildings. Deborah Sussman, principal of Sussman/Prezja & Company, began her career working with Charles and Ray Eames and soon became one of the West Coast's best known designers, recognized especially for her colorful, exuberant wayfinding programs.

Several dedicated environmental graphic designers with decades of experience, such as Wayne Hunt, Chris Calori, and Lance Wyman, serve as the vanguard of wayfinding education. While individual courses offer students insight into the profession and the challenges of wayfinding design, most students need

to supplement their knowledge before entering the field or joining a firm at an entry-level position. A solid educational foundation in wayfinding balances good communications skills—graphic design, typography, layout, and information design—with basic training in three-dimensional design for the built environment and an understanding of the materials and processes used in industrial design. Work experience or an internship in the industry, such as at a printing or fabrication company, can also be invaluable. If a young designer is ambitious enough to establish a company, a familiarity with the diversity of subjects offered by a university education or advanced-degree program can be greatly advantageous, as are post-graduate or continuing-education courses in management skills.

Even established design firms constantly refine their approach to wayfinding by researching new technologies, working in new parts of the world with different cultures, or just embarking on increasingly challenging programs. By tackling ever-larger projects, firms can become more adept at planning and strategizing, the core skills of good wayfinding design. And as each new staff member brings unique experience, understanding, and ideas to bear, so do clients, collaborators, and fabricators. Expertise in wayfinding design ultimately grows more from experience than from a specific education or career path.

WORKING AS AN ENVIRONMENTAL GRAPHIC DESIGNER

Wayfinding designers organize themselves in several different ways depending on scale of operation. Typically, they are members of medium- or large-sized consulting firms in which creative work consumes a majority of the energies of the staff. Some designers work in small firms with only two or three employees, fostering an "all hands on deck" culture where everyone shares responsibilities. There are also environmental graphic design departments within architectural firms that function almost like independent contractors, developing signage systems for the parent firm and for outside clients as a separate profit center.

Straightforward projects can be handled by a small studio with just a few people involved. Large projects requiring more complex teams are usually undertaken by bigger design companies, often in partnership with other firms. Executing these complex projects may require collaborators, either from inside the firm or outside experts hired for specific tasks, such as strategists to help analyze a situation, map makers and illustrators to create special pieces of artwork, and traffic engineers and technical specialists to create design documentation.

Small Project

Regional theater company's new home

This design team is small and streamlined. Responsibilities are shared, and the designers maintain close contact with the client without intermediaries. The client group is also small and functions as an advisory review committee for the project manager. The consulting architect, who may be a collaborator, client, or just an advisor, reviews the signage program during development to see that it conforms to the design intent of the building.

THE CLIENT TEAM

Theater Founder and President

Marketing Director

Artistic Director

Project Manager

THE BUILDING ARCHITECT

Architecture Firm

THE SIGNAGE DESIGN TEAM

Creative Director

Project Designer

Production Designer

Medium Project

Urban biotechnology research campus

The design team is larger and more formalized in a medium-sized project. Each team member has a specific role, and lines of communication are more clearly drawn. The client group may still be small, but there are other players at the table, such as a creative consultant who is responsible for ensuring that his corporate client's design standards are followed. Because this is an urban project sponsored by an economic-development department that represents the city's interests, the client and design team ultimately report to this department. The city art review commission has a stake in safeguarding the design integrity of the civic streetscape. Architects and landscape architects work on major aspects of the project's design. And for special landmark signs—a feature element of the site design—a signage fabrication company has been retained to serve as a design-build consultant.

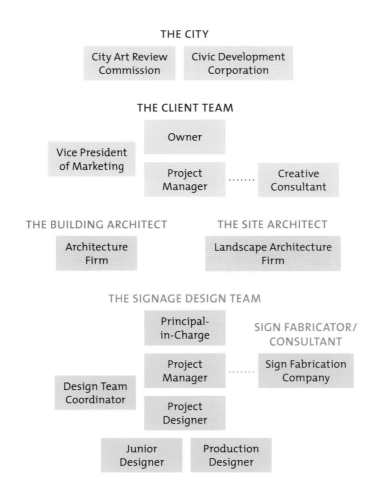

THE CITY

| City Art Review Commission | Civic Development Corporation |

THE CLIENT TEAM

Owner

Vice President of Marketing

Project Manager .... Creative Consultant

THE BUILDING ARCHITECT
Architecture Firm

THE SITE ARCHITECT
Landscape Architecture Firm

THE SIGNAGE DESIGN TEAM

Principal-in-Charge

SIGN FABRICATOR/ CONSULTANT

Project Manager .... Sign Fabrication Company

Design Team Coordinator

Project Designer

Junior Designer   Production Designer

Large Project

Professional football stadium

By virtue of their complexity, large-scale projects often have many participants at the client level who need to provide input and approvals. As this top-heavy chart shows, the new stadium will be home to two sports teams, each with multiple owners and the executives who report to them. A regulatory commission, in this case a state development agency, oversees the design and construction of the new stadium. The building-design team ensures that the stadium's architecture, interior design, sponsorship signage, and wayfinding program are all carefully planned and integrated. A large environmental graphic design team, with its own hierarchy of managers, specialists, and designers, executes the wayfinding strategy by developing final designs and supervising their implementation.

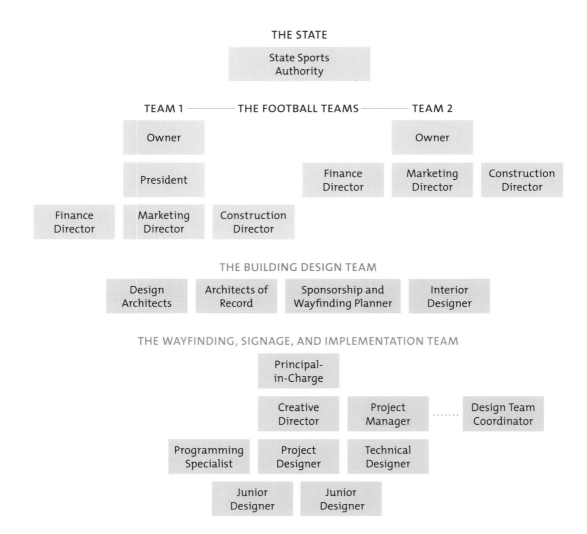

THE STATE

State Sports Authority

TEAM 1 ———— THE FOOTBALL TEAMS ———— TEAM 2

Owner

Owner

President

Finance Director

Marketing Director

Construction Director

Finance Director

Marketing Director

Construction Director

THE BUILDING DESIGN TEAM

Design Architects

Architects of Record

Sponsorship and Wayfinding Planner

Interior Designer

THE WAYFINDING, SIGNAGE, AND IMPLEMENTATION TEAM

Principal-in-Charge

Creative Director

Project Manager

Design Team Coordinator

Programming Specialist

Project Designer

Technical Designer

Junior Designer

Junior Designer

The Design Educator

The environmental graphic design profession is such a vibrant, growing field that there is a much greater demand for young designers than the marketplace can supply. Firms compete for the limited number of design school graduates who have the necessary wayfinding or signage background and often have to spend several years training in-house staff before they can manage teams or work on complex projects. Since its founding, the Society for Environmental Graphic Design (SEGD) has addressed this problem in part by connecting professionals with teachers and students and by producing workshops, conferences, research papers, and publications.

SEGD's ultimate academic mission is to develop full-fledged partnerships with university design departments in order to build environmental graphic design (EGD) courses into their curricula, ultimately making it a concentration. Before focusing on a subject as specific as wayfinding, students need to learn fundamentals of communication design, particularly typography and branding identity, as well as three-dimensional design. And while the ascendancy of computers has rendered the technical drawing skills previously taught in trade schools obsolete, students should

still learn drawing for concept development purposes to be able to explore ideas in a fluid and expedient way.

Our goal is to develop integrated programs with dedicated, full-time professors who hire experienced professionals as visiting or adjunct lecturers. The programs will offer EGD courses in the third and fourth years of a student's studies or at the graduate level alongside more standard concentrations such as illustration, industrial design, or package design. We also encourage collaboration with architecture or planning departments to fully round out an EGD education. After developing proficiency in foundational skills, students can explore specialized subjects that may vary depending on the institution but will likely include wayfinding, branded environments or placemaking (see chapter 3.1), and exhibition design. The type of programs offered by Kent State and Drexel University are successful models because they attract many EGD practitioners to teach on a rotating basis, which is more powerful than having one person repeat a subject year in, year out. University programs encourage students to concentrate less on learning technical skills, such as developing a sign message schedule, than on becoming strong conceptual thinkers and communicators—before joining a firm, graduates need to know how to write a concept statement, con-duct research, and put a design brief together as much as how to develop technical drawings or plan complex systems.

Firms today compete in two ways: by offering either a higher level of design or more efficient services. We aim to help our membership achieve both of these goals by building better academic programs and by fostering design leadership through increasingly sophisticated educational offerings.

Craig M. Berger is director of education and professional training for SEGD and editor of the book *Wayfinding: Designing and Implementing Graphic Navigational Systems* (2005).

2 PLANNING WAYFINDING SYSTEMS

2.1 THE DESIGN PROCESS

Function is fine but designers as the artists of our system must,
as it were, provide the spice as well as the nutrition.
ALAN FLETCHER

Each design project is a unique assignment with designated team members, special logistical and technical
requirements, and distinct design goals. There are,
however, predictable steps that define the process of
wayfinding design. Understanding this procedure helps
the designer—and the client, for that matter—succeed.
As the designer gains experience, he or she will be able
to complete more projects efficiently and profitably.

?

LEARN ABOUT
Each phase in the design process
and the products delivered

The process chart on the following pages provides a general template for how most wayfinding projects proceed once the design firm is awarded a contract. In smaller projects phases are sometimes combined or even eliminated. At times several phases of a job may have to run concurrently to accommodate a rush schedule. For long-term projects, there may be pauses between stages when the architects or project planners execute work that must be completed before wayfinding design can continue. The chart describes the typical steps in the design process and the usual order in which they are undertaken.

Each phase in this chart is addressed in greater detail later in the book; chapter references appear at the bottom of each column. It also briefly describes the designer's typical deliverables—the presentations and products that designers create throughout the life of the project. Unusual or special projects follow variations on the standard process.

 ## The Wayfinding Designer

When I became an environmental graphic designer about twenty years ago, designers still wrote out type specifications for outside typesetting services and produced technical drawings by hand. The standardized process we follow for wayfinding design, however, has changed very little because our work phasing follows the time-tested process established by architects (see chart on pages 34–35).

We now spend more time at the front end of a new project on planning, which requires understanding the client's goals and the needs of the end-user, and studying the unique wayfinding challenges presented by a specific site or building. This planning work involves research, meetings, site visits, and analysis of information such as circulation patterns. Our firm focuses on the strategic aspect of planning: confirming a clear set of the design goals and recommending what types of signs will be necessary for better navigation. We act as the users' representative and try to understand a space or building from their point of view.

Other factors affecting the way we work today are the changing market environment and client expectations. State-of-the-art computer capabilities and competition for projects are forcing wayfinding designers to produce increasingly sophisticated presentations in addition to the standard realistic renderings, models, and prototypes. Architects have raised client expectations by presenting virtual environments that simulate the walk-through experience—animation and 3-D rendering may provide the new best way to demonstrate wayfinding.

Growing demand for sustainable design solutions (see chapter 3.6) influences materials selection and even the scale of a sign program. While it's often best to minimize the number of signs in a program, specifying too few may require building staff to implement wasteful quick-fix solutions and actually add more signs in the long run.

As a mature EGD firm we work on large, complex way-finding projects that require design solutions with timeless appeal and long-term durability. A team might be involved in a sports-stadium project for several years after the de-sign strategy has been established. These types of projects offer the opportunity to affect thousands if not millions of people. The work is rewarding, but it requires time and patience to collaborate with the client's team until consensus is reached. When a number of these long-term engagements are running simultaneously, the ability to keep track of concurrent assignments at different phases is essential. An interest in graphic design, architecture, sci-ence, branding, and materials is also indispensable—not to mention the ability to read a scale ruler!

Anthony Ferrara is the creative director at Two Twelve Associates.

The Design Process

Planning			Design
RESEARCH & ANALYSIS	**STRATEGY**	**PROGRAMMING**	**SCHEMATIC DESIGN**

Hold project kickoff meeting, conduct user interviews, focus-group meetings, and site surveys to understand operational requirements and other demands the wayfinding system must address. For any new construction, review architectural plans and analyze anticipated circulation patterns. Identify exterior vehicular and pedestrian traffic flows and interior pedestrian patterns for key user groups. Determine user patterns and needs to establish the basis for the design program. Describe the problem to be solved.

Based on results from the research-and-analysis phase, propose a strategy for the wayfinding system. This strategy will be the functional framework for the system, explaining how it will provide information and directions for a place and how it will address user requirements. Develop an outline of the types of signs that will be needed. Establish the design goals for the signage system. A clear and effective strategy will provide the basis for successful signage.

With sign-type strategy established and circulation paths anticipated, consider critical decision points and other key locations requiring signage. Plot each sign location on a plan. Create a draft of the message-schedule database with all sign texts entered. Use this database to calculate and budget preliminary sign fabrication costs. By the end of the project—during design development or documentation—complete messages can be recorded and final sign locations noted.

Select key sign types and explore design alternatives, varying the forms, materials palettes, color, typography, and content. All options should conform to the wayfinding strategy but investigate different approaches to content and visual vocabulary. Identity and branding design may occur at the beginning of schematic design. By the end of this phase, the design vocabulary should be established, and design direction approved.

DELIVERABLES

• Project schedule • Research report and site observations • Problem statement	• Wayfinding strategy • Design goals • Outline of sign types	• Draft sign location plans • Draft sign message schedules • Preliminary sign fabrication budget	• Identity or branding design recommendations • Approved approach to the design vocabulary using selected sign types

TO LEARN MORE SEE:

2.2 Planning and Strategy

2.2 Planning and Strategy
2.3 The Categories of Signs

2.4 Sign Content and Locations

3 Wayfinding Design

DESIGN DEVELOPMENT

Develop the approved schematic design scheme to resolve details of typography, color, materials, finishes, and mounting for the wayfinding program. Finalize designs for each sign type and get client approvals. Coordinate with the architect and engineer about power requirements, structural issues, and architectural integration. Revise the sign-fabrication budget now that the sign quantities are fixed and the details resolved.

CONSTRUCTION DOCUMENTATION

Create design-intent drawings for all of the approved sign types. Create final sign layouts, elevations, and fabrication details to define design intent. Write sign specifications to describe the design-intent standards and all special requirements. Assemble or complete the final sign location plans and sign message schedules.

BID SUPPORT

Identify and contact qualified sign fabricators. Hold a prebid meeting or conference call to explain the project, discuss the design-intent documents, and answer any questions. Throughout the bidding process, provide clarification of the design-intent documents as necessary. Once the fabricators have submitted bids, assist the client with their evaluation and the selection of a bidder based on qualifications and price quotation.

CONSTRUCTION ADMINISTRATION

Attend a preconstruction meeting to clarify the design-intent documents for prospective bidders. Throughout the process, review fabricator submissions and answer any related questions. Make site visits to the chosen fabricator's workshop to review materials, colors, samples, etc. After fabrication is complete, provide supervisory assistance on site during installation. Inspect final installation and create punch list of necessary corrections and modifications.

DELIVERABLES

- Developed details of all sign types
- Refined fabrication budget estimate

- Design-intent documents
- Final sign location plan
- Final sign message schedule
- Sign specifications

- Bidders list
- Review services

- Clarification sketches
- Review services
- Punch list

TO LEARN MORE SEE:

3 Wayfinding Design
4.3 Code Requirements

4.4 Documentation and Fabrication

4.4 Documentation and Fabrication

4.4 Documentation and Fabrication

2.2 PLANNING AND STRATEGY

Just as this printed page, if it is legible, can be visually grasped as a related pattern of recognizable symbols, so a legible city would be one whose districts or landmarks or pathways are easily identifiable and are easily grouped into an overall pattern...
KEVIN LYNCH, *THE IMAGE OF THE CITY*

When people attempt to navigate a place for the first time, they face a series of decisions as they follow a path to their destination. There is a sequential pattern to this wayfinding process—in effect, a series of questions that people ask themselves along the way. Before starting the design process, the wayfinding consultant must anticipate visitor patterns, understand that logic, and apply it in the planning phase. Then work can begin on a framework for the wayfinding design program.

?

LEARN ABOUT
The development of effective
wayfinding strategies

APPROACH, ENTER, FIND

Imagine you are a visitor looking for a museum in the cultural district of a large city where many buildings have the same architectural style and look alike. You approach one, feeling a mixture of hesitance and excitement: Am I going in the right direction? Is this the museum I want to visit? If the old main door looks closed, you might be confused about how to enter the building: Should I enter by that new side door next to the parking lot? And once inside: How do I find the Renaissance painting exhibit?

At each stage in this sequence, the visitor must make decisions based on the available, and readily visible, information. The job of the wayfinding designer is to present information in public spaces that helps facilitate a seamless visitor experience. In other words, the necessary sequence of movement should feel as effortless and simplified as possible so that ten steps, for instance, seem to require only two or three.

The designer's challenge is to determine where to locate signs, what they should say, and how they should say it. Thoughtful research and analysis help the designer understand a complex public place, such as a century-old hospital campus or a huge urban subway system. In the process of tracing the visitor's path, the designer attempts to uncover the hidden logic of the place. Once that is clear, the designer can develop a strategic framework for the wayfinding system.

FOUR WAYFINDING STRATEGIES

The wayfinding strategy is the idea or system that underlies the design of a signage program. A strategy might help define the lines of a transportation network, the wings of a building, the neighborhoods of a city, or the precincts of an academic campus. There are four types of strategies that organize most wayfinding systems. These strategies are modeled after urban planning: the concepts of districts, streets, connectors, or landmarks can all be used to help make places easier to understand and navigate. For instance, district systems are pervasive: a place is divided into meaningful zones for use on signs and maps, and specific destinations are clustered within those districts. Where streets provide the wayfinding metaphor, easily recognizable corridors and pathways form a comprehensible network across a space. Connectors are simple bold pathways that connect all of the destinations within one location. Landmark strategies direct people to major nodes, like elevators or primary destination points. In order to understand these contemporary wayfinding concepts, it is useful to look at urban history to see the inspiration for these ideas.

HISTORIC URBAN MODELS

Cities are by their very nature complex places, dense with people and the different neighborhoods where they reside and work. An understanding of how cities evolved systems that organize or define their social and geographic structures is essential for effective wayfinding practice.

The Forbidden City in Beijing exemplifies an urban microcosm carefully planned to convey a specific message. Built in the early decades of the fifteenth century, the palace housed the Chinese imperial court. The form and layout of the palace complex was rigidly axial and highly symbolic: its high, imposing walls,

The Forbidden City, Beijing, China (Connector model)

concentric system of gateways and courtyards, colors, materials, and place names all communicated the court's power. For those outside the Forbidden City's walls, the architecture and the urban design symbolized power and dominance. For those allowed entrance, the succession of courtyards and palaces clearly led the way to important central destinations. The strong central axis through the palace complex was a connector linking the world outside to the emperor. Though the fabric of Beijing is being torn apart today to accommodate extraordinary growth, the integrity of the Forbidden City's plan survives.

University of Cambridge, United Kingdom (District model)

Examining a medieval cityscape reveals a very different kind of spatial organization. The University of Cambridge grew during the thirteenth century in the heart of a then-small city northeast of London. Town and university mingled together into a complex thicket of meandering streets, the result of the city's evolution from Roman outpost to Norman settlement to medieval university town. Cambridge, like its great rival in Oxford, evolved into a network of colleges within the larger

university framework. This system of residential and academic colleges, each with distinct names, coats of arms, defined precincts, and specific gateways, was a kind of early campus wayfinding, a mechanism of organizing the puzzle of Gothic buildings into coherent understandable entities.

Rome, Italy (Landmarks model)

During the baroque period, Pope Sixtus V had a vision for recapturing Rome's ancient glory. In order to create a grander setting for the seat of the modern Catholic empire, and help pilgrims find their way, the pope conceived an urban master plan for the city. His system of axial roads and landmark focal points structured future growth and development. The center point of each axis indicated the location of a major civic landmark. In some cases Egyptian and Roman monuments were relocated to these places to define them, in others, extant ancient churches were remodeled in the baroque style. These landmarks survive in situ today, a testimonial to Sixtus's innovations that established a distinct pattern for future urban development of this great city.

New York, New York (Streets model)

By the nineteenth century, as cities became larger and more complex, planners proposed new systems of organization to cope with growth. The Commissioners' Plan of 1811 for New York City, a remarkable document that shaped the city's growth, relied upon a deceptively simple wayfinding mechanism for understanding the urban layout: the grid of numbered streets and avenues. The result is that contrasts in New York are dramatic; for example, areas of Lower Manhattan that inherited the footprint of its colonial-era settlements have a confusing, if charming, tangle of streets. Further north, a grid of numbered streets and avenues takes over, and wayfinding becomes clear and understandable. While the intersection of Nassau and Pine streets down in the Financial District sounds mysterious, most out-of-towners are able to find Fifth Avenue and Fifty-fourth Street very easily.

EARLY MODERN URBAN WAYFINDING

With these systems for organizing urban space in mind, it is instructive to take a closer look at some of the visual and conceptual communication devices that cities have adopted over time. In Beijing, specific colors helped to define the imperial precinct. Red and yellow were reserved for the emperor's use and signified the majesty of his Forbidden City. In Cambridge, coats of arms represent each of the colleges, creating a shorthand for identifying different parts of the university.

Starting in the second quarter of the nineteenth century, German publisher Karl Baedeker set the standard for tourists' travel guides with his authoritative books

Coats of Arms, University of Cambridge

filled with notes about destinations, routes, and ratings for attractions. Shortly after the widespread availability of the automobile, André Michelin's guides for the new automobile owners, likewise, provided a narrative of the important destinations that travelers would encounter on a trip to Rome, for example. These guides and their

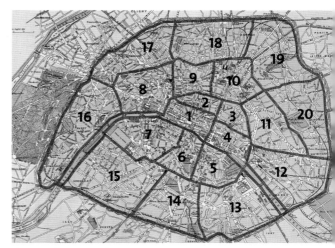

The arrondissements of Paris

imitators have provided a worldwide reference for finding destinations and landmarks within the tangle and mystery of foreign cities.

Civic planner Baron Haussmann used bold strokes in mid-nineteenth-century Paris when he modernized the city by introducing a system of radial boulevards. He also created arrondissements, or districts: spiraling concentric city zones that provided a shorthand way for Parisians and visitors to dissect the city into

Paris street sign

areas they could remember and find easily. Over time these districts developed specific social and cultural meanings. Additionally, distinctive, artful signs, introduced in the nineteenth century, show the street name and the arrondissement number and are as fundamental to the Parisian streetscape as the Eiffel Tower.

When the United States Post Office established zip codes, another pattern of boundaries was superimposed over New York's street grid. These codes facilitate mail and parcel delivery, but they also convey social information. Having a specific zip code indicates economic status—10021 or 10065 on the Upper East Side imply wealth and social distinction—as do neighborhood names such as Carnegie Hill.

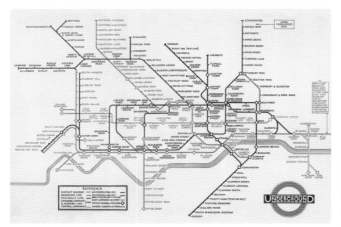

London Underground Map, 1933

Most large environmental graphic design projects begin with research, when the wayfinding team studies a site in detail to identify the populations that inhabit the place, pathways that they follow, any obstacles to good wayfinding, and opportunities that might promote it. The site investigation involves observation and documentation, walking the streets or corridors, and looking at landmarks, pathways, and gathering points. While exploring a space, the designer observes its physical characteristics and the human dynamics that take place there. This may include studying typical circulation patterns for different populations and what kind of information they need. In addition, complete research also requires plan reviews—a detailed study of the architectural drawings of a building or complex—and constituent interviews.

In the second half of the nineteenth century, metropolitan railroads began to connect city dwellers to workplaces and recreational destinations. By the early twentieth century, these railroads came together to form mass-transit systems. As these systems grew after the turn of the century and the public needed help deciphering routes, map makers began to color code the different lines. Harry Beck's precedent-setting map design for the London Underground, issued in 1933, changed transit maps forever. He organized the spaghetti of routes into a system of lines all drawn at consistent angles. He structured the typography over a grid and noted the station interchanges symbolically. This brilliant map codified and abstracted spatial information, foreshadowing contemporary wayfinding systems and, curiously, also recalling the rigid geometry of the Forbidden City (see chapter 3.4).

Depending on the time and budget available for research, as well as project priorities, interview subjects may include facility operators, program managers, senior executives, and security guards. This process uncovers additional details and the peculiarities of a place—problems and opportunities that may exist but are not visible from mere observation. It is important that the designer understands how people experience or are expected to experience a place. Using data gathered during interviews, as well as notes from site surveys and plan reviews, the designer then diagrams people's movements. Pathways and decision points become obvious in the process, and issues of identity and image are also revealed.

THE RESEARCH PROCESS

The historic examples of urban coding methods previously described typify systems that early city planners created to organize and communicate aspects of urban infrastructure. These methods provide models for the modern wayfinding designer to use to organize signage programs for various types of spaces. These coding systems are applied only after initial planning to determine the most appropriate wayfinding approach for a particular project.

Depending on the nature of the place—be it a city center, a new corporate building, or an existing institutional campus—the focus and depth of wayfinding research will vary. For existing spaces being re-signed, the study focuses on what is already in place, how it works, where the problems are, and what changes need to be implemented. For new facilities, the research reveals how the place will appear to the user and how it is expected to function.

User Circulation: Corporate Technical Center

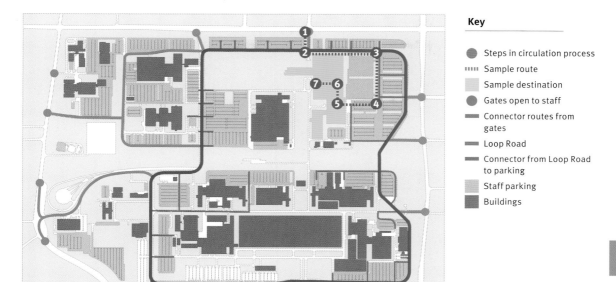

Key

- ● Steps in circulation process
- ▪▪▪▪ Sample route
- ▢ Sample destination
- ● Gates open to staff
- ▬ Connector routes from gates
- ▬ Loop Road
- ▬ Connector from Loop Road to parking
- ▢ Staff parking
- ■ Buildings

The circulation diagram shown above shows the analysis of circulation by a particular user group, in this case staff coming to the corporate technical center. Interactions at each step in the process are described. This scenario is one of several done for different user groups. A review of the parallels, overlaps, and contradictions between the different user pathways shows the designer how to assess the need for visitor information at the center and how to develop a wayfinding strategy.

1. Employee enters at a gate, noting the number on the entrance sign and the hours of operation on the regulatory sign.

2. Employee drives on Loop Road and follows vehicular directional signs to the final destination.

3. Employee sees the appropriate parking-lot directional for the destination building and turns off of Loop Road.

4. Employee enters assigned parking lot, which is marked with building name, lot identification signs, and row markers.

5. Employee enters building at card-key staff entrance where minor building identification and door-regulatory signage is present.

6. Upon entering that building, the employee sees and follows building directories and/or interior directionals.

7. Employee proceeds to the workspace that is signed with the appropriate floor, room, and column identification.

SITE ANALYSIS

Having looked separately at different constituencies and their pathways, the designer next develops summary maps of the overall circulation patterns. On an outdoor campus, vehicular and pedestrian movement might be mapped separately to show the different experiences each entails. With this information the designer can establish a family of sign types and devise a site-specific wayfinding strategy.

The two drawings on the facing page describe the pedestrian and vehicular wayfinding systems for the Princeton University campus by showing the movement of people and cars and the location of arrival places and decision points. The designer examines these diagrams to create a set of wayfinding recommendations and a strategy for the placement and content of signs. The pedestrian drawing shows the east–west walkway system as a full-fledged campus circulation network; the vehicular drawing depicts a system in which visitors are directed along the central roadway and then separated into east and west circulation and visitor parking systems. A picture begins to emerge.

 The Campus Planner

OTHER VOICES: NEIL KITTRIDGE, AIA, AICP

As campus planners for Princeton University, our team works independently of the many architects hired by the admin-istration to design buildings. While Princeton selects world-class architects who do innovative work, each one of them grapples with a unique set of constraints. Our job is to provide objectivity and continuity and to make sure that every building fits into the campus as a whole. The same principle holds true for working with a wayfinding team.

The ideal campus wayfinding consultant works collaboratively and designs with a very light touch. After interviews and visits to the campus, our wayfinding team identified different features about Princeton's landscape that particularly help people find their way around. We had interesting debates—everyone has a different idea about how the campus should be organized, whether by neighborhood, topography, or historic period—but in the end we came to consensus about what works. Since the wayfinding program needed an organizing principle, we chose Princeton's beloved system of established circulation pathways, or "walks," as the framework upon which to organize all future development. Because of this structure, new buildings will be better sited and more accessible from key circulation routes.

Given a choice, architects, planners, and administrators would probably do away with signs completely! But after an unembellished presentation proved just how hard it is for visitors to find the admission's office, the administration appreciated the need to improve campus wayfinding. While eliminating signs entirely was unrealistic, we kept signage to a minimum by introducing visual prompts into the landscape to make movement more intuitive. New public buildings and structures were sited to function as arrival landmarks and gateways, while the campus landscape was refined to open up and highlight Princeton's system of walks, which serve as important pathways for pedestrian movement.

Our end product is the Princeton Campus Plan, a report that will guide development for at least ten years. Using the term *master plan* tends to be problematic today because it suggests that everything has already been worked out, without flexibility for unanticipated changes. We prefer the idea of a framework—an armature upon which everything hangs—to describe planning guidelines based more on a philosophy than on hard-and-fast rules. This approach serves a major institution much longer and more effectively than a traditional master plan.

Neil Kittredge, AIA, AICP, is partner and director of planning and urban design for Beyer Blinder Belle Architects & Planners LLP.

Pedestrian and Vehicular Strategies: Princeton University

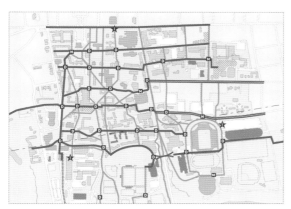

Pedestrian Wayfinding Diagram

- ⬤ Major campus destination
- ★ Visitor information kiosk
- M Campus map case
- D Pedestrian pathway directional
- ▬ Primary pedestrian route
- ▬ Secondary pedestrian route

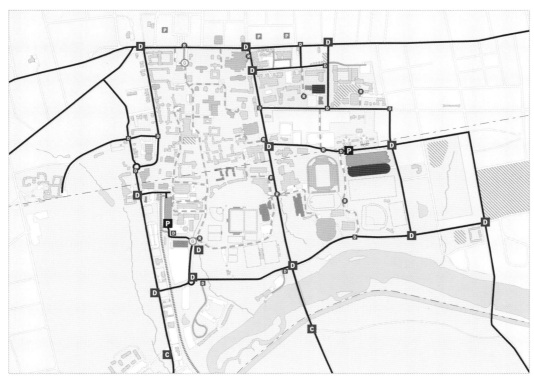

Vehicular Wayfinding Diagram

⬤ Primary campus destinations	C Campus identification	P Visitor parking	▬ Primary roads
D Major directional	R Restricted access sign	P Pay-to-park (off-campus)	▬ Campus driveways
D Secondary directional		G Campus guard booth	▬ ▬ Restricted-use campus roads

FINDING THE HIDDEN LOGIC

Synthesizing research is critical for effective wayfinding design. By reviewing architectural plan information such as that shown on the previous pages—site observations, interview data, and user circulation studies—the designer seeks to uncover "the hidden logic" of a place. This hidden logic is the pattern of movement or spatial organization that characterizes a place and serves as a framework for the wayfinding system. As discussed at the beginning of the chapter, there are four main types of wayfinding strategies, based on connectors, districts, landmarks, and streets.

These strategies are, in essence, different types of mental maps, simple diagrammatic views of complex places that people grasp and understand quickly and easily. Designers use these maps or frameworks to structure a system of signs that will help people navigate, depending on the strategy, from district to district, along streets or corridors, or between landmarks. The strategy is revealed both graphically, on signs, and spatially, through the architecture, to people where they enter the system at one or more arrival points. The system then leads people on to further decision points. These examples demonstrate how these strategies actually work in contemporary environments (see also Children's Hospital Boston case study on pages 60–62 in chapter 2.4).

**A Historic City
(Districts model)**
City Founder William Penn laid out the city of Philadelphia on a rational grid in the late 1600s. When creating a pedestrian wayfinding system for the historic city center more than three hundred years later, the designer embraced Penn's four quadrants and the adjacent historic waterfront area, created names and symbols for them, and used these historic districts as the cornerstones of a pedestrian signage program.

APPLYING THESE STRATEGIES TO A HOSPITAL CAMPUS

The map (right) shows the buildings and corridors of the Johns Hopkins Medical Campus a large, urban academic medical center. The diagrams (opposite) show options for using different wayfinding strategies to organize the hospital signage program. These demonstrate the four basic strategic concepts described previously. Option 1 highlights a connector that ties the hospital complex together, leading patients and visitors to the different buildings. Option 2 divides the hospital into districts, geographic clusters of buildings that are named and color-coded. Option 3 treats the individual building elevators as destinations or landmarks. Option 4 is based on the streets model; with named corridors.

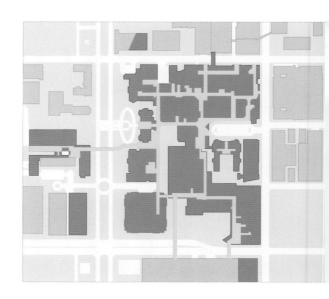

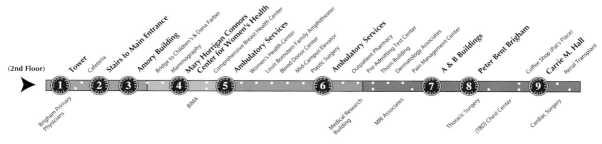

(2nd Floor)

Tower — Brigham Primary Physicians
Cafeteria
Stairs to Main Entrance
Amory Building
Bridge to Children's & Dana Farber
Mammography — BIMA
Mary Horrigan Connors Center for Women's Health
Comprehensive Breast Health Center
Ambulatory Services
Women's Health Center
Louis Bornstein Family Amphitheater
Blood Donor Center
Mid Campus Elevator
Plastic Surgery
Ambulatory Services — Medical Research Building
Outpatient Pharmacy
Pre-Admitting Test Center
Thorn Building — MRI Associates
Dermatology Associates
Pain Management Center
A & B Buildings — Thoracic Surgery
Peter Bent Brigham — (TBD) Chest Center
Coffee Shop (Pat's Place)
Carrie M. Hall — Renal Transplant / Cardiac Surgery

Hospital (Connector model)

At Boston's Brigham and Women's Hospital, the main connector was named the Pike, a spin on the Massachusetts Turnpike, familiar to most state residents. Access points to buildings became numbered "exits" on the Pike.

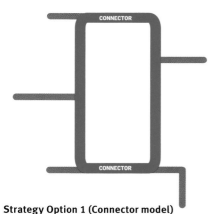

Strategy Option 1 (Connector model)

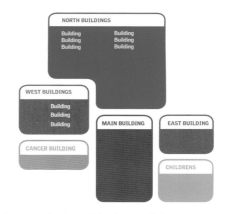

Strategy Option 2 (Districts model)

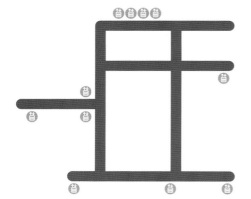

Strategy Option 3 (Landmarks model)

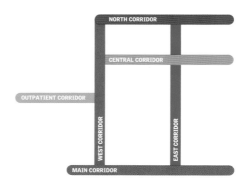

Strategy Option 4 (Streets model)

2.2

2.3 THE CATEGORIES OF SIGNS

Signs are necessary in innumerable ways. Their mission is either one of social function or of economic necessity…The general arrangement of both public and private signs should have a character and an expression that is congenial to and beneficial for the individual and the community.

MILDRED CONSTANTINE, *SIGN LANGUAGE FOR BUILDINGS AND LANDSCAPE*

A wayfinding system links different people together, even if they do not share a common language or destination, by guiding all of them through the same space with a single system of communication. The unifying language of a wayfinding system creates a public narrative of how people witness, read, and experience a space. Each sign in a system, each separate voice, serves a particular function and displays a specific kind of content called a *message*, which might include nonverbal graphic symbols, images, and words.

? LEARN ABOUT
Different types of signs most wayfinding programs require

The narrative is the voice of the building and that of its owner, revealing the pathways and destinations of the building or space, the rules that govern how to use it, and essential information about activities happening within. It is the job of the wayfinding designer to weave these voices together into a single eloquent statement as people navigate the space.

Most wayfinding systems can be broken down into several categories of signs: identification, directional, orientation, and regulatory. This section will explore the variety of signs used in wayfinding design and how they can accentuate impressions about a place. Donor recognition signs, often included in many large wayfinding programs, are employed where there is a compelling need to acknowledge the individuals who have made it possible to build and fit out a new institutional facility. In the interest of brevity, and because donor signs serve a different function than the other elements of the wayfinding program, that category is not presented in this chapter.

The pictoral essays on the following pages offer a glimpse of the diversity of sign types found around the world. Vernacular signs that are not "designed" in the professional sense are often very effective in a local context but are not included in these visual surveys.

Sign Types List

For an indoor retail center with on-site parking

Exterior

IDENTIFICATION
Site monument identification
Site entry identification
Building mounted identification
Entrance identification
Parking area identification
Accessible parking identification

DIRECTIONAL
Off-site trailblazers
On-site vehicular directional signs
Pedestrian directional signs

REGULATORY
Parking regulations
Entrance information

Interior

IDENTIFICATION
Store identification
Area/Level identification
Public amenity identification
Service and maintenance identification
Office identification
Elevator and stair identification

DIRECTIONAL
Directional signs

ORIENTATION
Mall directory
Elevator/Floor directory

REGULATORY
Fire egress maps
Life safety signs

Identification Signs

The building blocks of wayfinding, identification signs often provide the first impression of a destination. These signs are visual markers that display the name and function of a place or space, whether it is a room, an individual building, or a campus gateway. They appear at the beginning and end of routes and indicate entrances and exits to primary and secondary destinations.

While identification signs clearly mark transitions from one type of space to another, their purpose is not purely functional. Styled appropriately, they also express a place's personality, character, and even its historic context. These signs can communicate a place's identity explicitly by presenting an actual logo or more generally by evoking an image.

Minnesota Children's Museum
St. Paul, Minnesota

LAX Airport
Los Angeles, California

Incheon International Airport
Incheon, South Korea

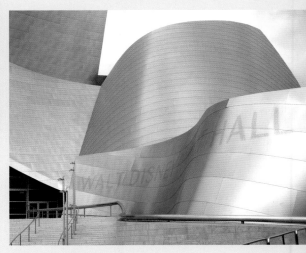

Walt Disney Concert Hall
Los Angeles, California

Heimbold Visual Arts Center
Sarah Lawrence College
Bronxville, New York

City Museum
Melbourne, Australia

HP Pavilion at San Jose
San Jose, California

Terror Háza Múzeum
Budapest, Hungary

Metro
Paris, France

Directional Signs

Directional signs constitute the circulatory system of a wayfinding program because they provide the necessary cues that users need to keep on the move once they have entered a space. This sign type routes pedestrian or vehicular traffic between main entrances, key decision points, destinations, and exit points by displaying graphic prompts, such as typography, symbols, and arrows. While their design should harmonize with the surrounding architecture, directional signs also need to be obvious and recognizable. Message content should be simple, coordinated for easy navigation through an entire facility, and based on a specific wayfinding strategy.

Streetscape
Norfolk, England

Roppongi Hills
Tokyo, Japan

Melbourne Docklands
Melbourne, Australia

British Museum
London, England

Eureka Carpark
Melbourne, Australia

Düsseldorf International Airport
Germany

Shea Stadium
Queens, New York

Orientation Signs

To make a complicated space less baffling, orientation signs offer visitors an overview of their surroundings in the form of comprehensive site maps and directories. The design of orientation signs needs to coordinate with other identification and directional signs in a system. When all these signs work together, visitors are able to move easily along circulation routes.

Most site maps show people their location with a You Are Here indicator. Orientation signs in a multilevel structure often display a plan map (axonometric or flat, see chapter 3.4) of the pertinent floor. Outdoor maps show the boundaries of a campus, entryways, major buildings, or other components of the space. On directories, occupants are usually listed in either alphabetical or numerical order. Other methods of categorization, such as by use or tenancy, can be helpful. In most cases, maps should maintain the same orientation throughout a facility to avoid confusion. In buildings where occupancy changes are likely to be frequent, designers often utilize electronic or digital sign technologies that allow names and other information to be easily and economically updated without returning to the sign fabricator.

Orientation signs are usually large freestanding units readily visible to many people simultaneously, or wall-mounted if space does not allow. An exterior orientation map can also show how an entire site fits into the neighborhood or district context.

Information kiosk
Toronto, Canada

Airport directory
Ottawa, Canada

Park map
Grand Canyon National Park, Arizona

Downtown map
San Antonio, Texas

Exhibition hall directories
Yokohama, Japan

City orientation kiosk
London, England

Campus map
Austin, Texas

Regulatory Signs

A regulatory sign describes the do's and don'ts of a place. It can be as simple as a No Smoking sign or a more complex display with rules indicating how citizens should enjoy and respect their public park. Some regulatory messages, particularly those that describe egress from a building, need to comply with legal codes. As codes vary from one jurisdiction to another, it is important to become familiar with local regulations that apply to the site under consideration.

Regulatory signs should be unobtrusive and enhance the experience of a place but large enough to communicate instructions or warning information immediately. The writer needs to craft the language carefully, clearly stating the intent without making the visitor feel unwelcome. When the regulatory signs are well integrated into a sign system, they seem an essential part of the overall experience of place and not just a necessary evil.

Bakery
Thornhill, Ontario

Yale University
New Haven, Connecticut

Chicago Park District
Chicago, Illinois

Diemerpark IJburg
Amsterdam, Netherlands

London Underground
London, England

Tate Modern
London, England

Please!
No fishing
on this pier.

Fishing permitted
only on Fishing Pier 4.

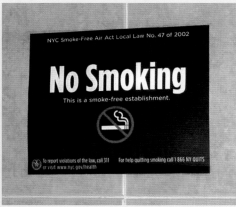

NYC Smoke-Free Air Act Local Law No. 47 of 2002

No Smoking
This is a smoke-free establishment.

To report violations of the law, call 311   For help quitting smoking call 1 866 NY QUITS
or visit www.nyc.gov/health

Restaurants
New York, New York

Queens West Development Corporation Parks
Long Island City, New York

2.4 SIGN CONTENT AND LOCATIONS

The new time sense of typographic man is cinematic and sequential and pictorial.
MARSHALL MCLUHAN, *THE GUTENBERG GALAXY*

Once analysis and strategy phases are complete, the designer then determines how to fit signs into a total system. This process, called *sign programming*, entails generating a database of messages (actual text on signs) and the specific locations of all signs necessary for a particular building, complex, or campus. Sign programming is not to be confused with architectural programming, which determines the functional elements of a building—a related but different activity. To program messages and locations, the designer establishes the specific sign types the project requires and analyzes circulation patterns into, around, and through the site. Having established sign locations and functions, the designer drafts the actual message copy. This chapter covers the task of locating signs and developing a message schedule and contains a more general discussion of sign content.

? **LEARN ABOUT**
Creating sign content and choosing installation locations

PLANNING SIGN LOCATIONS

Sign programming begins with an analysis of arrival, departure, and decision points; circulation pathways; and signing opportunities. Depending on the project, the designer either proceeds with a list of sign types established by the client or uses the analysis process to generate one. To avoid problems later, it is essential that the designer survey a building or a space exhaustively to become completely familiar with the territory. The initial list may contain more signs than are ultimately necessary, but it is safer to overestimate and edit later.

The designer marks up architectural plans with possible sign locations and then creates a database of signs. Using a coding system to assign a sign type to each location, the designer also enters the actual message—either a word or a phrase—associated with each sign. In the early stages of data entry, some messages are just placeholders until copy is finalized. Sign locations may also be approximate when the building is not yet fully detailed or a final location is still in question. This early work is called *preliminary programming*; the later work, when messages and locations are all confirmed, *final programming*.

Typically, the first pass at programming occurs before any signs have been designed, but sometimes it is necessary to create diagrams of the sign types for presentation purposes or to help the programming process. These diagrams make it easier to explain to a client or stakeholders group how the signage system will work. The case study on pages 58–59 shows the elements in the signage programming process: the list of sign types, sign elevations, a sign-location plan, and a sign-message schedule.

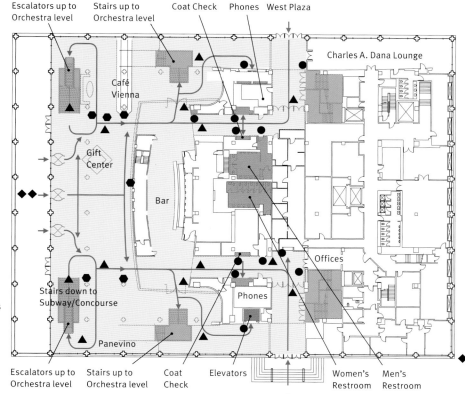

Circulation Analysis
This diagram shows the circulation analysis for the ground-floor entry of a large concert hall. The red line delineates projected circulation pathways, while the different symbols indicate the kind of information and sign type required at each point. Once all floors have been surveyed, the requirements of the sign system come into focus, and actual signage programming can commence.

(ID=Identification signage)
◆ Exterior building entrance IDs
● Interior building & level IDs
● Room & space IDs
▲ Interior directional signs
— Pedestrian circulation

Escalators up to Orchestra level · Stairs up to Orchestra level · Coat Check · Phones · West Plaza

Charles A. Dana Lounge

Café Vienna

Gift Center

Bar

Stairs down to Subway/Concourse

Phones

Offices

Panevino

Escalators up to Orchestra level · Stairs up to Orchestra level · Coat Check · Elevators · Women's Restroom · Men's Restroom

SIGN-PROGRAMMING CASE STUDY

These examples typify sign-programming documents created for a small urban bus terminal: a list of sign types, sign elevations, a sign-message schedule, and a sign-location plan. Red and blue highlights track how two signs in the group are represented in the different contexts.

Sign Elevations

These are elevation drawings of selected sign types in the program (ID=Identification):

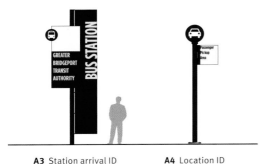

A3 Station arrival ID   **A4** Location ID

List of Sign Types

This list is broken down into the categories of signs: identification (ID), directional, and regulatory.

A1   Primary station ID—facade mount
A2.1 Primary station entrance ID—overhead wall mount
A3   Station arrival ID—post mount
A4   Location ID—post mount
A5   Bus berth ID—canopy mount
A6   Window ID—overhead wall mount
A7   Room ID—wall mount
A8   Closet ID—wall mount
A9   Egress stair ID—door and wall mount
A10 Restroom ID—wall mount
A11 Amenity ID—flag mount
B1   Directional—wall mount
B2   Directional—overhead wall mount
B3   Directional—overhead ceiling mount
B4   Directional—canopy mount
B5   Directional—strap mount
C1   Station regulatory—silk screen
C2   Regulatory—door mount
C3   Regulatory—post mount
C4   Regulatory—strap mount
C5   Regulatory—wall mount

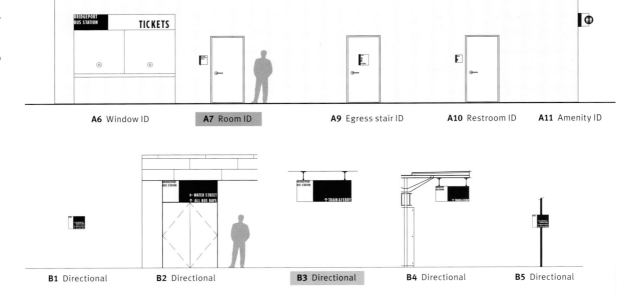

A6 Window ID   **A7** Room ID   **A9** Egress stair ID   **A10** Restroom ID   **A11** Amenity ID

B1 Directional   **B2** Directional   **B3** Directional   **B4** Directional   **B5** Directional

sign type	number	side/panel	arrow	messages	remarks	reference
B2	105	S1-P1	↑	Exit to Water Street Passenger Pick-up Area	Directional *Overhead wall mount*	See A1.962
C5	106	S1-P1		(Regulator Message TBD)	Regulatory *Wall mount*	See A1.962
A2.2	107	S1-P1	↑	Bridgeport Bus Station Connector Entrance	Small entrance ID *Overhead wall mount*	See A1.962
C1	108	S1		(Station Open Hours Message TBD)	Station regulatory *Screen printed*	See A1.962
B2	109	S1-P1	↑	Exit to Water Street Passenger Pick-up Area	Directional *Overhead wall mount*	See A1.962
B3	110	S1-P1	↑	Ticketing/Information Waiting Hall Elevator to Train & Ferry	*Directional* *Overhead ceiling mount*	*See A1.962*
		S2-P1	↑	Exit to Water Street Stair to Train & Ferry		
C5	112	S1-P1		(Regulatory Message TBD)	Regulatory *Wall mount*	See A1.962
A7	113	S1-P1		(Room number TBD) (Identification Message TBD) [Braille]		See A1.962

Sign-message Schedule

To the left is an excerpt of the sign-message schedule. It shows several records in a database format. These are the headings and descriptions of the data fields used to record information: sign type (reference code of actual sign type), number (actual sign location), side/panel (side or panel with message), messages (actual sign text), remarks (sign type and mounting information), and reference (page number in drawing package of sign illustration).

Sign-location Plan

Below is the ground-floor plan of the bus terminal. Each sign type and number is noted in a box, and a line connects that box to the sign's location on the plan.

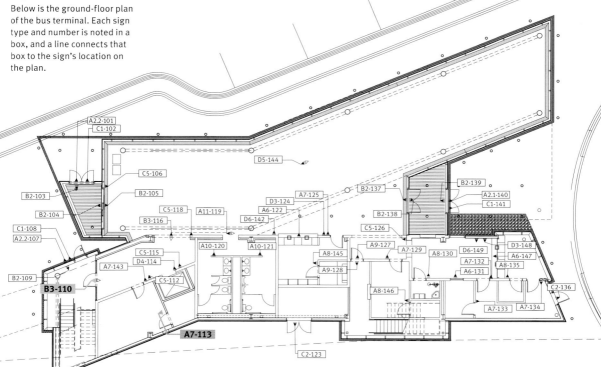

Children's Hospital Boston, Wayfinding with Districts and Connectors

Sign Content and Locations

2.4

Planning and Wayfinding Systems

The experienced wayfinding designer plans the sequence of signs in a space and crafts understandable messages for these signs so that visitors can successfully find the destinations they are seeking. This case study shows how the messages are displayed on key sign types in the signage program for a complex academic medical center. The system for Children's Hospital Boston is based on a wayfinding strategy that designates the five interconnected principal hospital buildings as color-coded districts and employs their three lower floors as connectors to link all these buildings. Wayfinding information is organized hierarchically as follows:

- The five buildings (districts)
- Primary destinations (admitting, blood donor)
- Secondary destinations (meeting rooms, exam rooms)
- Public services (restrooms, telephones)
- Other rooms (offices)

Each sign type has been designed to hold a different category of message in specific places. This flow of information on signs will help to guide people's wayfinding process into stages: First, direct people along the connectors to one of the districts; concurrently, provide directions to the primary hospital destinations. Within the districts, provide elevator directories to upper-floor destinations and directional signs pointing to all destinations within the district on that floor. Finally, mark the individual rooms with a system of identification plaques.

The Hospital Buildings
The diagram above shows the five principal hospital buildings, the number of floors, the color codes, and the three lower floors that function as connectors.

Coding the Buildings
The system of symbols, names, and colors that are used to code the different buildings in the hospital is depicted below.

Hat = Hunnewell = Red

Fish = Fegan = Teal

Flower = Farley/Pavilion = Yellow

Boat = Bader = Green

Moon = Main = Purple

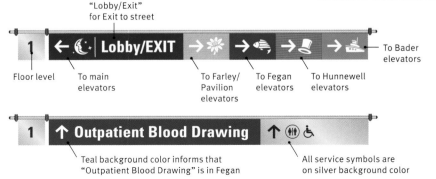

"Lobby/Exit" for Exit to street

Floor level   To main elevators   To Farley/Pavilion elevators   To Fegan elevators   To Hunnewell elevators   To Bader elevators

Teal background color informs that "Outpatient Blood Drawing" is in Fegan

All service symbols are on silver background color

Overhead Directional Signs
The three connector floors of the hospital have overhead directional signs that guide people to individual buildings and their elevators as well as to primary destinations and services. On the connector, signs help patients, families, staff, and other visitors navigate the horizontal connectors of the hospital.

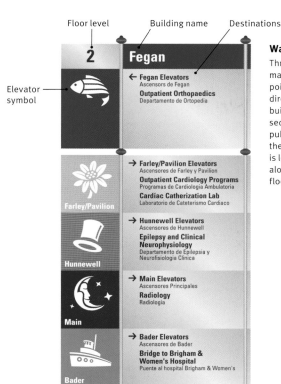

Floor level · Building name · Destinations

Elevator symbol

Wall-mounted Directionals

Throughout the hospital at major intersections and decision points, there are wall-mounted directional signs that list building names, primary and secondary destinations, and public services. The name of the building where the sign is located appears at the top along with its symbol and floor number.

Elevator Directories

Once they arrive at a desired elevator bank, visitors consult the elevator directory to locate the level they need. When they reach that floor, the secondary wall directionals will lead them to their final destination.

Building abbreviation · Room number

Braille

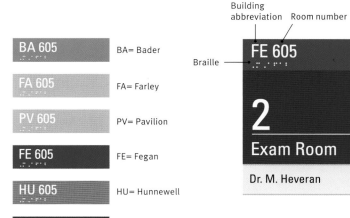

BA = Bader

FA = Farley

PV = Pavilion

FE = Fegan

HU = Hunnewell

MA = Main

Room-identification Plaques

The top portion of all room plaques is color coded according to the building's designated color and indicates the name of the department or room number in Braille. The two-letter abbreviation is a special code that refers to the building where the sign is located. Royal blue is the standard base color for all sign plaques.

Children's Hospital Boston, Signage

Lobby Sign (left)

The letter *G* at either end of this large overhead sign in the main lobby indicate the ground-floor location. Symbols, building names, and arrows in color-coded boxes direct visitors to the actual building locations.

Directionals on the Connector (below)

Overhead signs direct visitors to buildings; wall directionals guide visitors to buildings and major destinations found along the connector. A wall directional header indicates the first-floor Farley/Pavilion location.

Overhead Sign on the Connector (above)

This simplified overhead sign displays just the building symbols and colors as well as major nearby services. A large 1 indicates the first-floor location.

Identification Sign (right)

An overhead sign identifies the outpatient X-ray department in primary (English) and secondary (Spanish) languages. Purple indicates the department's location in the Main building.

UNDERSTANDING SIGN CONTENT

The programming of sign locations and messages requires answering specific questions: Where are people going? Where do they need information? How can verbal signs help the wayfinding process? In many cases drafting the sign message is simply a matter of recording a room's function or its occupant's name. In others, it is a more complex matter of anticipating needs and interpreting communication requirements. For complicated situations the designer uses the wayfinding strategy as a guide to creating messages for signs. Simplicity is the best approach; symbols are great shorthand for quick messaging.

In increasingly multicultural American cities, it is often critical that signs be bilingual. Selective translation is a powerful way to communicate to minority populations and make everyone feel welcome. In truly bilingual environments, signs have to be designed to carry the two languages side by side. To understand this process, first look at simple examples, and then move to more complex situations as illustrated in the identification- and directional-sign case studies that follow.

MESSAGES ON IDENTIFICATION SIGNS

Identification signs are the simplest and most obvious sign type. The large exterior sign for a museum usually displays just the name of the institution—MoMA QNS, for example. A building identification sign for the Yale University campus indicates the name of the university, the building or department name (primary message),

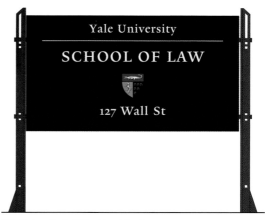

Yale University building identification

the address, and school shield. The location of information on the sign and its typographic treatment gives hierarchy to the message.

The courthouse room-identification plaque (below) is a simple interior sign stating just the room name and number and a simple regulatory message. Planning information hierarchies is critical when there are several levels of content, such as for an office-identification sign (below) in a federal courthouse, that require a number of layers of information: the judge's name and title, the federal court system to which he or she belongs, and the room name and number. Interior information signs must also conform to the Americans with Disabilities Act (ADA) requirements (see chapter 4.3).

MoMA QNS site identification

Courthouse room identification

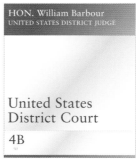

Courthouse office identification

Massachusetts General Hospital suite ID

Massachusetts General Hospital floor directory

the elements of the Shea Stadium sign. The orange and blue are the team colors that appear on the sign for Gate B. (Gates range from A through E in this stadium.) Orienting seating sections to the bases is an easy way to communicate in the language of baseball: for instance, Gate B falls near Third Base. Seating in large stadiums and performance venues is often divided into sections of odd and even seats. To further clarify the location, a plan is color coded to indicate the levels of seating. The You Are Here indicator points out the location of Gate B. The ballpark signage engages fans by referencing the familiar conventions of baseball parks to help them find their way.

MESSAGES ON DIRECTIONAL SIGNS

Other identification signs rely on different strategies to define their content. At Massachusetts General Hospital's outpatient building, address codes were developed for the individual clinics in the ten-floor building. The names for the different clinics are sometimes quite complex, combining the medical specialty with the donor name. The sixth-floor directory (left) lists the clinics on that floor and cross-references them to the address codes, 6A, 6B, 6C, and so on. Bold perpendicular flag signs (above left) at each clinic's door display its address. More detailed naming and patient information appears on the glass next to the door. As discussed on pages 50–51, directional signs primarily guide people to specific destinations or clusters of destinations. An example from Montgomery College (opposite top) shows how a simple

Shea Stadium gate identification

An identification sign for Shea Stadium (right) is necessarily very different. In a large baseball park, signage needs to help people find their seat among the thousands in the stadium quickly. A number of conventions that define ballpark seating determined

exterior sign can direct vehicular traffic to different buildings on campus. Pedestrian signs for the Chicago Park District (bottom right) provide directions to various destinations: sign panels shaped as long arrows with a symbol and message point the way to the different locations. No strategies here, just directions.

The wayfinding system for downtown Baltimore (below) has several layers of information. The area is divided into several districts, each named and assigned a distinctive color: The area markers for the Mount Vernon Cultural District are burgundy-colored. A symbol for the downtown wayfinding system is mounted to the district-marker panel. The panel with directions is divided into two sections: the blue area has directions to individual destinations and to other districts, and the green area gives directions to nearby public-transportation facilities.

Simplicity is the best approach to planning messages for signs. Context often offers cues to the right method, and with some reflection, the appropriate solution usually presents itself. For complex environments, logical strategies provide a guide to designing clear and understandable messages when the task of wayfinding seems overwhelming.

Montgomery College vehicular directional

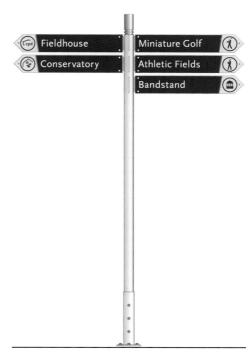

Chicago Park District pedestrian directional

Downtown Baltimore wayfinding

Notruf
Nothalt

MVG Kundencenter
SWM Shop

WC Marie...

...thalt

...hr am Zug
...leisbereich
...tehen!

...otruf

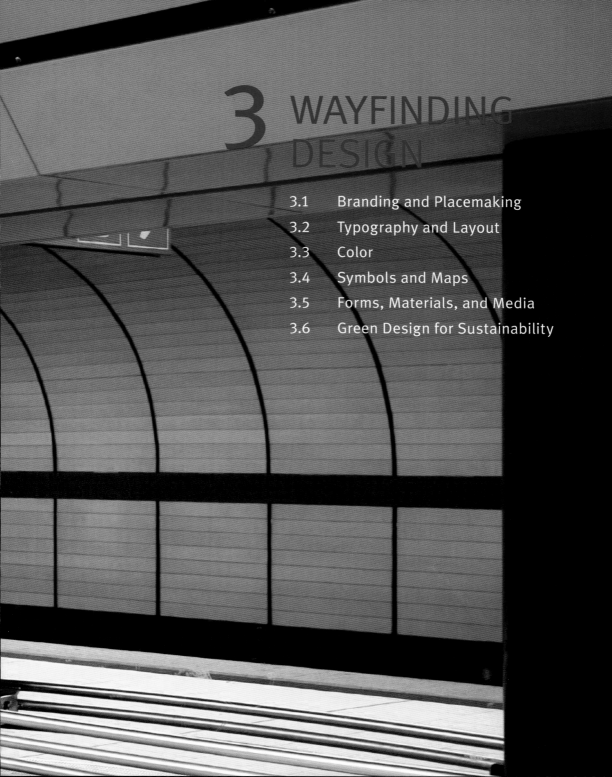

3 WAYFINDING DESIGN

3.1 BRANDING AND PLACEMAKING

This above all: to thine own self be true,
And it must follow, as the night the day,
Thou canst not then be false to any man.

WILLIAM SHAKESPEARE, *HAMLET*

Strong brands drive today's consumer economy. Companies routinely invest huge amounts of time and creative resources to develop a vocabulary that familiarizes consumers with their products and services. Branding fosters awareness, enthusiasm, loyalty, and participation. In recent years branding has also been embraced by cities, cultural organizations, and institutions not traditionally associated with this kind of marketing approach. As brand concepts become richer, complex, and more broadly applied, designers' skills and strategies require greater sophistication. Environmental graphics and wayfinding design have become powerful tools to help build or enhance both public and private brands, from universities and oil companies to civic downtowns and modern Olympiads.

? LEARN ABOUT
How environmental graphic systems can build brands, create identities, and establish a sense of place

THE LANGUAGE OF BRANDING

Before branding became ubiquitous, most marketing strategies emphasized a memorable logotype as the mainstay of an identity-design project. Even today a logo is often the most important expression of a corporate or product identity. One glance at the Coca-Cola logo, for instance, is enough to evoke the brown soda's fizz and bite or the sensation of a cold drink after a hot day. Decades of advertising campaigns have reinforced iconic images of the classic bottle and the signature curvaceous graphic swash.

Color conveys equally powerful and specific associations. The rich robin's egg blue of Tiffany & Co. suggests the imminent presentation of an engagement ring or some other precious object. A bag, box, or catalog in this signature color automatically raises the prospect of a luxury gift.

There was a time in the late 1990s when an ad or billboard needed just three simple words—Just Do It—to mean Nike. The campaign for Air Jordans and scores of other futuristic running shoes made them seem so essential that enthusiasts flocked to the bright new Nike stores in droves, driving a rapid expansion of the chain in cities across the United States and abroad. These throbbing marketplaces quickly became exciting urban destinations where fans grooved on images of their heroes while trying on the latest sportswear.

Consumers in a simpler era needed only a painted sign on the side of a barn describing their favorite brand to prompt a visit to the country store for a tin of Mail Pouch tobacco. Families traveling by car through the United States in the 1930s enjoyed the "experience" of Burma-Shave signs along their route. These familiar white-on-red signs were installed as a procession of four, five, or six messages. One would appear, then another, playfully leading to the punch line: "His cheek was rough/His chick vamoosed/And now she won't/Come home to roost/Burma-Shave." These campaigns

were so influential that the Burma-Shave trademark transcended its association with men's brushless shaving cream and became a code word in the sign trade for an installation of signs or messages that run in sequence.

BRANDING A WAYFINDING SYSTEM

Environmental graphic designers face different scenarios when they consider how to integrate branding with wayfinding for a client's project. In some cases an existing brand strategy or identity must be applied to a new sign program. The client provides guidelines for using an existing logo, verbiage, fonts, colors, symbols, and any other proprietary or "signature" brand elements, and the designer must determine when and where it is appropriate to apply these to signage and make recommendations for adjustments or substitutions. If certain messages, fonts, colors, or layout schemes are not suitable for large-scale or three-dimensional applications, the designer may need to argue for changes or additions to the brand strategy and palette to keep signage in compliance.

In other cases the designer creates a new brand identity in tandem with a new wayfinding program. This clean-slate situation is optimal because it ensures that all branding elements will be coordinated with the signage and allows the designer to create a more holistic brand experience. This rebranding process usually involves a more diverse client team than a discrete signage-design project would, including management, marketing, and communications departments in addition to people representing facilities, architecture, and landscape design. This broader involvement, while harder and more expensive to manage, can result in a more widely adopted brand strategy as well as a more coherent and unified public image.

In either case the designer should think of the merger of wayfinding and branding as environmental placemaking. Though building an identity for a place usually starts with a logo, either preexisting or newly minted, a complete wayfinding program offers much more substance. Comprehensive branding of a place folds in messages, shapes, materials, forms, and media as well as human factors like staff presence or appearance. Well-conceived wayfinding programs not only define a space but also make it appealing and coherent for customers or visitors.

HOW DOES BRANDING WORK?

The case studies that follow show how effective environmental graphics can be in supporting a brand and establishing a sense of place. Representing a variety of clients and settings, these strategies also demonstrate how a place or experience can be made uniquely memorable. While subsequent chapters in this section will explain specific wayfinding design elements in greater detail, these studies show how all the parts fit together.

Apple Stores

Architecture and attitude express the brand

Since they first opened in 2001, Apple stores have become a remarkable phenomenon, contributing to the enduring popularity of the company's line of computer and entertainment products. The stores mirror the products: smart, elegant, and user friendly. Featuring a large-scale Apple logo simply placed at the center of the facade, the stores boldly announce themselves without words. Inside, the neutral white interiors present a high-tech gallery setting for a product line that is both the message and the medium. Shoppers can seek technical support at the Genius Bar or consult with a Creative at the Studio for help. Each gesture is carefully designed and executed, but the overall effect is one of effortless simplicity and minimalism.

BP

The oil company with a different voice

BP is the world's second-largest company in the business of drilling for oil, refining it, and selling it and one of the largest gas retailers in the United States. Though still primarily in the oil-and-gas business, the company has created a complementary identity that highlights its support of the environment, alternative energy sources, and green living. This notion of branding with a conscience starts with the logo—a green-and-yellow sunflower—and extends to the company's public-relations message about environmental values and sustainability. These colors pervade the gas stations and dominate company advertising. BP also commissioned the design of Helios House, a striking, "green" gas station in Los Angeles made of recycled aluminum, the first ever to be to be submitted for LEED certification in the United States (see chapter 3.6).

(RED) Campaign

Global branding for a cause célèbre

An offshoot of the ONE Campaign that hopes to unite Americans "to help make poverty history," Product (RED) is the brainchild of rock star Bono and his colleagues. The purpose of the licensed, red-color logo—used by corporate partners on their products in exchange for 50 percent of the profits—is to attract consumer attention and dollars to African AIDS victims. While ONE focuses on influencing long-term policies, (RED) is intentionally a quicker fix with huge publicity value. In a matter of months, the list of partners included Gap, American Express, Apple Computer, and Emporio Armani. People began to see (RED) everywhere, permeating advertising, products, and events, such as a free concert in London's Trafalgar Square celebrating a new Motorola phone product.

Yale University

Campus wayfinding and brand expression

Yale University relies on simple yet powerful graphic devices to express its prestigous brand. So-called Yale Blue is one of these tools, the family of coats of arms is another, and, of course, the famous name itself. As part of a campaign to unify all university communications, Matthew Carter created a typeface with several variations, including one for signage applications called "Yale Street." The wayfinding program, developed to welcome visitors, further supports the image of prestige. The signpost design is a contemporary take on Collegiate Gothic, the architectural style of many of Yale's important buildings. Sign panels present the main branding devices: name, color, typeface, and shield. In this case wayfinding becomes a multipurpose tool that reinforces institutional identity, presents a more welcoming environment, and fosters goodwill through a more accessible campus.

Downtown Brooklyn

Pedestrian wayfinding and borough branding

Brooklyn used to be one of the largest cities in the United States. Now part of New York City, the borough has undergone a remarkable transformation in the past decade since its downtown was revitalized. The old Brooklyn was a commercial center surrounded by residential neighborhoods. Today, Downtown Brooklyn is coming to be known as a significant destination, where some twelve neighborhoods intermix business and commerce. The Downtown Brooklyn pedestrian wayfinding program unites these neighborhoods more directly into a cohesive and walkable urban center while also enhancing the identity of Downtown Brooklyn. A cheeky abbreviated logotype, an idiosyncratic bent and folded sign profile, a striking color palette, useful directions, and informative maps express the brand.

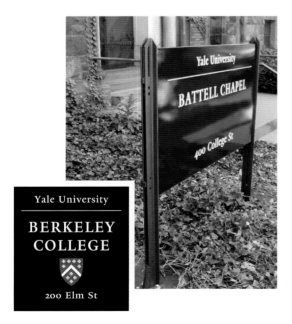

The Design Strategist

Branding is all about the ability of an enterprise to successfully deliver on promises made to the public, whether they come in the form of a guarantee of a high-quality product or a first-class education. The best branding programs take advantage of every opportunity to identify the enterprise represented and articulate its core values, mission, and offerings.

That's why branding today is a multidisciplinary pursuit that goes much deeper than just creating an effective logotype and a memorable tag line. Effective branding addresses all aspects of corporate or institutional culture, including the public face presented by staff and their working environment.

How does wayfinding relate to branding? As a design strategist, I help institutions communicate with constituents who come to their campus or facility by developing comprehensive visitor-service programs. These clients need to understand that anything visitors experience or encounter should express their brand. For instance, a website is a particularly important branding tool because it helps people form an impression about a place before they actually visit it. When they approach the site, graphic prompts and other signals can confirm that they've actually arrived. Coordinated

symbols, colors, names, signage, architecture, and landscaping together reinforce the institutional identity and express a specific sense of place, of being somewhere in particular. The practice of branding an environment to feel distinctive is also known as placemaking.

Just as the discipline of branding supplanted identity design some time ago, experience design is the next important professional specialization that has evolved to help enterprises differentiate themselves. Apple's popular iPod and iPhone are good examples of experience design because they invite the user to listen, communicate, and interact with them. This concept applies to wayfinding because environments and signage must be designed with the user in mind, otherwise the visitor experience is just about getting lost!

Some institutions, particularly universities and hospitals here in the east, are a little reticent about embracing contemporary strategies such as branding and experience design, but most appreciate the need to emulate practices that are standard in the commercial world. Cultural venues are way ahead of the curve—a perfect example is the Smithsonian Institution's National Museum of the American Indian (left), where everything a visitor encounters is appropriate and coordinated, from the native food served in the cafeteria to the stone selected for the building. Any enterprise that pays careful attention to every detail of the customer experience will have visitors who are happier, and who have better first and last impressions. Today, that matters.

Sylvia Harris, an expert in public-interest branding and information design, is well-known for her leadership of the 2000 Census redesign and communications strategies for NewYork-Presbyterian Hospital, the American Civil Liberties Union, and Columbia University.

3.2 TYPOGRAPHY AND LAYOUT

A letter has no fixed shape, it does not even have a skeleton shape, it has identity, and this exists in the mind.
NICOLETE GRAY, *A HISTORY OF LETTERING*

Looking at the evolution of environmental graphic design over the past four decades, it becomes obvious that great typography dominates many successful projects. The monumental sign for the Talleyrand Office Park is iconic, the simplest and boldest of typographic statements. Equally dramatic is the innovative facade of the Lucent Technologies Center for Arts Education at the New Jersey Performing Arts Center—the transformation of a conventional early-twentieth-century school building into one gigantic mural of text. Signage for the Berlin subway system, also beautiful and memorable, presents complex transit information with precise, elegant clarity.

LEARN ABOUT
The elements of good typography for wayfinding

What makes these environmental graphics so appealing? Just the choice of typeface, or also how it is interpreted in context, scale, color, form, or materials? In fact, all of these considerations come into play. The designer who strives for typographic excellence—the foundation of a classic graphic design education—can elevate otherwise mundane signing into an iconic statement, something instantly recognizable and closely associated with a specific place. Careful letterform design and expressive typography can make all the difference between delivering a mediocre solution or an outstanding one.

The designer's basic typographic tool kit consists of twenty-six letterforms, ten numbers, and necessary punctuation in English, accent marks and characters depending on the language. A skilled typographer—today the term refers to a designer who works with type rather than an independent typesetter—weaves all these elements into a tapestry of messages that make a place more accessible. He or she follows a multistep process involving typeface selection, letterform scaling, and panel layout. Excelling at type layout for signage requires the ability to prioritize information into logical hierarchies based on time-tested rules of typography. Experience and training help build these skills, but having an innate talent for evaluating letterforms or a good eye for proportion does not hurt.

ARCHITECTURAL LETTERING EVOLVES

The earliest evidence of wayfinding design survives today in the form of architectural inscriptions that identify buildings and monuments as important landmarks or destinations. The legacy of carved letterforms, pictographs, and imagery is a story unto itself, a journey through time and space. These "signs" were produced by artisans to communicate civic messages or religious teachings. The ancient Egyptian ruling classes used hieroglyphics to celebrate the accomplishments of royalty and their dynasties. During the classical period, Romans created the forerunner of our alphabet, still visible on thousands of public buildings and monuments. A Roman inscription is bold, strong, and clear—an indelible mark intended to rally the subjects of a vast empire. Likewise, Mayans illustrated narratives

Egyptian hieroglyphics

Roman inscription

Mayan glyphs

of conquest and power on their temples and stelae using a unique written language and number system. In Europe, the lettering on tombs inside Gothic cathedrals complements the detailed tracery of the architecture and mirrors the curvilinear calligraphy of the monks recording sacred knowledge in the Middle Ages.

By the nineteenth century, with the rise of the modern capitalist industrial era in Europe and North America, commercial and civic signs competed for attention in the public landscape. The teeming mid-

century urban streetscape of New York and other large American cities became an extraordinary catalog of signs plastered across the facades of buildings advertising the enterprises within. Their letterforms were rarely uniform; instead commercial letterers drew them from scratch to reflect the style of the decade and tastes of the owner, often forcing the designs to fit a given space. Though this typographic cacophony may seem a visual feast to today's audience, it was considered an eyesore at the time, the sign of a mercantile society run amok.

During the first half of the twentieth century, when corporate moguls commissioned increasingly tall buildings and architects shaped early skyscrapers, type was often integrated into the building fabric. Names intended for permanence were either inscribed directly onto facades or incorporated into metalwork and other decorative detailing on exteriors and interiors. This lettering complemented the architectural style of the buildings, often with powerful and extraordinary results.

By the late twentieth century, facilities sprawled rapidly and demand for comprehensive directional sign systems grew. Visitors required increasingly sophisticated graphic signals and prompts to find their way through ever larger and more complex public spaces. Today, cities, corporations, public events, or transportation systems not only need wayfinding programs to communicate public information clearly and directly, but also to express a brand image that distinguishes them from the competition. Signage demands may have become more complicated, but now typographic options are limitless, offering exciting creative opportunities. This chapter guides the designer through the process of selecting typefaces for wayfinding signage and using them successfully.

CHOOSING A TYPEFACE

The beginning of the design process is the time to explore type families and select the appropriate typeface to suit a specific site and context. It is difficult to imagine today that in the 1960s and '70s a single typeface, Helvetica, was used almost exclusively for most sign systems. Classically trained graphic designers otherwise relied on a vocabulary of about a dozen "acceptable" typefaces. Evolving tastes, the broadening of cultural and social perspectives, and personal computers loaded with digital type soon changed everything. With type fonts now numbering in the thousands, the wayfinding designer has to develop an even more discerning eye to balance issues of form versus function.

Typefaces have specific personalities and suggest certain associations: Bembo seems traditional; Meta appears crisp and modern; Ziggurat is playful. When selecting a typeface, the designer must consider how it will be used: Will it appear on a carved inscription, as dimensional letters, on an illuminated board, or on a map? Will it guide drivers on a highway, students through a university, or diners to a restaurant? The experienced designer instinctively understands the typographic requirements of a project and selects a font that is both appropriate and communicative.

COURTHOUSE
Bembo

RESTAURANT
Apex New

Hoefler

Amusement
Ziggurat

1053
Valuta

Museum
Avenir

University
Baskerville

INSTITUTE
Bell Gothic

BOTANICAL GARDEN
Requiem

&
Caslon

Freeway
Highway Gothic

Transportation
Meta

BALLPARK
Fairplex

Vialog

3.2

LETTERFORMS ON SIGNS

Individual letterforms are the basic units of the way-finding equation. Before diving into the discussion of typography for wayfinding signage, it is useful to identify the key elements of letterforms.

Serif letterforms

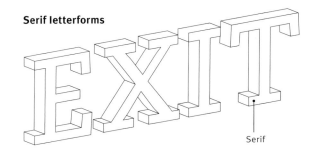

Serif

Sans serif letterforms

Cap height

X-height

Baseline

Ascender

Bowl

Counter space

Descender

The Type Designer

Before designing a typeface for wayfinding purposes, we ask for two types of feedback from the client or designer who represents them. The first is emotional or psychological, such as what qualities characterize the client's organization. The second, more importantly, is technical, which addresses all the practical aspects of the project. For instance, indoor public spaces often need illuminated signs, and backlighting a sign can play havoc with the interior spaces of letterforms. Although many sign systems appear to use only a single font, they actually rely on subtle variations of it in order to present a unified typographic voice for different contexts and sign material choices.

Our typeface design for Radio City Music Hall was inspired by the art deco signage that is unique to this site. This historic precedent was very helpful, but the original artists never designed a full alphabet. As a response we created a font based on these handmade fragments and added punctuation, numbers, and other missing characters. The challenge was to capture the spirit of the original lettering in a contemporary, systematic typeface that meets Americans with Disabilities Act (ADA) requirements. In the end we drew two fonts, one very narrow and the other very wide, in order to allow for words of different lengths to be set on signs of a given size. A well-designed typographic system lets the font do the heavy lifting: any need for manual intervention points to a problem with the font itself.

Letterspacing was more of an art thirty years ago, when the alphabets used by designers existed solely as physical artifacts that had to be carefully applied to specific media, such as photostats pasted on cardboard or letters mounted on walls. Contemporary fonts must be meticulously designed if they are to reproduce this level of craftsmanship without active involvement from a designer. Kerning is a good case in point: we take pride in figuring out every possible letter combination in advance, even obscure pairs, like *y* and *q*, to make sure they will mesh properly. This can add up to an extraordinary number of possible combinations: 676 for capital letters alone, and then caps to lowercase, lowercase to lowercase, and even the spacing between punctuation marks.

Legibility relies as much on the application of a typeface as it does on the design of the individual letters. We test our designs in a variety of situations in order to examine mechanics—consistency, color (varying tones of gray formed by the texture of the type), and fit. Legibility is certainly paramount, but it's difficult to measure scientifically. I have yet to see a really scientific, peer-reviewed, double-blind legibility study. Almost every signage project starts with the client, often an architect, requesting an all-uppercase solution, as if capital letters are somehow sturdier or safer! The reality is that lowercase letters are essential for text readability because they produce more distinctive word shapes, which is especially important in signage, where environmental factors come into play. For instance, an upper- and lowercase highway sign can often be read even when a bridge or other obstacle obscures the top half of the line.

I love handmade letters in part because good artisans have always understood both the microperspective of lettering and the macroperspective of words. For the type designer, nothing surpasses the envisioning of a holistic typographic concept for a specific situation where lettering is totally integrated with a design. Although creating a custom font for a signage program can be impractical, some projects still demand it. In the case of Radio City, the extant letters were so marvelous that building upon them was too good an opportunity to pass up. It was a true restoration project.

What wayfinding designers ignore at their own peril is considering the breadth of a type family. A single sans serif may be useful for a handsome sign prototype for which you can cherry-pick the copy, but it doesn't anticipate a later need to introduce secondary text or distinguish one type of sign from another. A signage program that's mated to printed communications requires even more typographic versatility, as do less glamorous signs like elevator indicators, which designers tend to ignore. My advice in picking a typeface for wayfinding is to try to plan ahead, or better yet, pick a typeface that plans ahead.

Jonathan Hoefler, president of Hoefler & Frere-Jones, is best known for the Hoefler Text family of typefaces, designed for Apple. In 2002 he received the prestigious Prix Charles Peignot award from the Association Typographique Internationale (ATypI).

OTHER VOICES: JONATHAN HOEFLER

CATEGORIES OF TYPEFACES

The inventory of typefaces is now so large that it is difficult to even categorize all the fonts available. The most basic differentiation is serif versus sans serif letterforms. Serif extensions at the end of a stroke are the legacy of the chisel mark and the swash of the calligraphic brush. Sans serif letterforms, which have unembellished stroke endings, matured in the early modern era in reaction to traditional styles. Slab serif fonts are a subset of serif types distinguished by bold, geometric endings on the letterforms—an evolution of popular nineteenth-century letterforms. Script typefaces mimic hand-drawn cursive letters. Decorative letterforms are self-consciously illustrative or eclectic.

Serif
Jenson

Sans Serif
Frutiger

Slab Serif
Geometric

Script
Snell Roundhand

Decorative
Raceway

Legibility Issues

Because signage must often be read at a distance by pedestrians walking quickly or passengers in moving cars, letterform legibility is critical to the success of a wayfinding program. Two important characteristics of letterforms affect the legibility of messages: the height of the lowercase letterforms, or x-height, and the openness of the voids inside the letters, or counter spaces.

High x-height
Dax

Low x-height
Futura

Open counter space
Akzidenz

Tight counter space
Vialog

Americans with Disabilities Act Compliance

The ADA defines parameters for selecting typefaces to ensure that they are readable for people with compromised vision. The ADA regulations require letters and numbers on signs to have a width-to-height ratio between 3:5 and 1:1 and a stroke width-to-height ratio between 1:10 and 1:5.

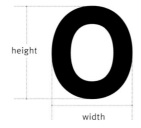

height / width

height / stroke width

1234567890
Aligning: Frutiger

1234567890
Aligning: Jenson

1234567890
Old-style: Scala Sans

1234567890
Old-style: Garamond, Old Style

The Numerals

There are two basic kinds of numerals: aligning and old style. Aligning numbers are the norm, but old-style figures can add a lyrical quality to a design as the numbers move above and below the x-height datum lines. Both serif and sans serif fonts sometimes offer these variations.

Choosing a Versatile Type Family

Examine a type family to see how much variation it offers in terms of slant, weight, and width. This is particularly important for wayfinding signage, where messages often appear in different settings and scales. Univers is a good example of a well-designed typeface that offers many different individual weights and letter types. The contemporary font Knockout is just that; countless subtle variations of stroke weight and width make it perfect for fitting a type message into a particular place or setting. Certain faces, such as Caslon, have a short lowercase x-height and offer small caps and old-style numerals, making them excellent choices for designs that need a classical or traditional look.

55 Roman
65 Bold
75 Black
55 Oblique
57 Condensed
53 Extended
Univers

UPPER CASE
Title Case
SMALL CAPS
Caslon

HTF30
HTF33
HTF50
HTF53
HTF68
HTF70
HTF73
Knockout

12" and up

4–5" minimum

2–3" minimum

Read

1/2"

Letters appear at 50 percent of actual size

TYPE SIZE AND ARRANGEMENT

Establishing the correct scale and arrangement of lettering for messages is key to good wayfinding design. The designer's goal is to make a sign system legible and flexible enough to accommodate a series of messages without looking confusing or chaotic. Having selected a typeface, the designer must then decide its size and weight. Context is critical in determining type size for signage.

These general categories provide one way to understand the relative sizes of letterforms and how they are used: reading, walking, driving, and environment. Reading letters are small enough to be used for text and captions on orientation-map kiosks or for narrative paragraphs on interpretive signs. Walking letters are of a size suitable for directional messages that guide pedestrians on city streets or in interior public spaces. Driving letters are large enough to be seen by drivers looking for directions or information. Several factors affecting these scale decisions for vehicular signage, such as the viewer's distance from the sign and driving speed, must be studied and tested during the design process. Environment letterforms are superscaled for maximum effect in busy urban streetscapes or on highways.

Line Length and Type Size

The line length of messages can also influence type size. For directional signs on a university campus or an urban wayfinding program, the designer can inventory all of the destination names and determine how the names will work on the signs, what line breaks are necessary, and where messages will need to be abbreviated. This process helps to establish what size lettering is appropriate for sign panels of a particular scale.

longest message

Engineering and Sciences

Greenleaf Hall

University Art Museum

Smith Campus Center

Letter Spacing or Tracking

Choosing the appropriate distance between letters, or tracking, is critical for maximizing message legibility. Generally, letters and words are spaced farther apart for signage application than in print media to enable messages to be read easily in extreme conditions or while moving. Light-colored type set against a dark background may need even looser spacing for the individual letterforms to remain distinct.

Type with Symbols and Arrows

Typographic messages often incorporate either a symbol modifier or an arrow for wayfinding signage. It is important to establish good scale relationships between these elements to ensure that the graphic mark and type read as a seamless unit and convey the intended message.

Line Spacing or Leading

Careful line spacing, or distance between lines, ensures that a series of messages can be easily read and understood without wasting or compromising space. It is important to group text appropriately, particularly in a narrow stack of names. In this case two-line names are tightly line spaced (A) while the spaces between names (B) are just generous enough to differentiate entries without making the overall list too long.

A **Performing Arts Center**

B **Mint Museum of**
A **Craft & Design**

B **Main Library**

B **Johnson & Wales**
A **University**

TYPE DESIGN FOR SIGN PANELS

Looking at actual examples is the best way to understand the rationale for type layout on signage. The panels shown on this spread represent a variety of venues, viewing conditions, and audiences. Their typographic styling takes into account legibility, branding considerations, and the architectural context.

Concert Hall Signs

These nickel-plated signs with glass panels have a simple, elegant design to match the neoclassicism of the music hall. They feature centered messages set in the typeface Requiem. Hairline rules with a decorative flourish separate the messages into a distinct hierarchy. The hall identification sign is modified by the name of the seating level in all capital letters. The gallery directory lists seating and services found on each level. The Founders Box identification plaque provides a large box number and, more modestly, the donor's name in italics.

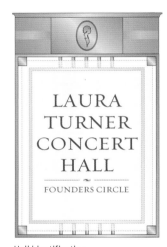

Hall identification

Gallery directory

Founders Box identification

University Signs

This example shows two sign types within one wayfinding system. The particular blue color and the Univers typeface are both the university standards. The typographic layout of the building identification sign is simple: the building name is flush left, with the university symbol in the lower right. The vehicular directional sign, scaled appropriately for drivers, guides visitors to major destinations. Arrows and L-shaped rules, or lines, provide directions to clusters of destinations.

Building identification

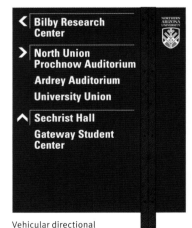

Vehicular directional

Park Signs

These signs belong to a city-park sign system. Color banding and material changes differentiate the backgrounds for different messages set in the Whitney typeface. On the identification sign the park name is prominent. The bottom band presents four types of information: symbols for available services, an advisory about closing time, city and park-system logotypes, and the slogan. The directional signs are similarly banded: The top displays an icon to indicate the audience, either pedestrians or drivers, and the main panel area shows destination information with an accompanying symbol—green symbols for parking and blue symbols for all others. Each bottom band reinforces the park brand or identity.

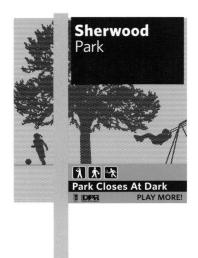

Park identification

Pedestrian directional

Vehicular directional

Stadium Signs

These sign panels, part of a large wayfinding program for a baseball stadium, are dense with information, including levels, numbered seating, and amenities. Appropriate to the ballpark setting, they also display team branding and sponsorship identification. The stair directory is a matrix that cues a level name to seating sections and amenities found there. A color highlight and a baseball signal You Are Here. The ramp-directional sign indicates the level and amenities ahead plus the way to the exit. The level-directional sign highlights seating sections and amenities.

Stair directory

Ramp directional

Level directional

3.3 COLOR

In order to use color effectively it is necessary to recognize that color deceives continually.

JOSEF ALBERS, *INTERACTION OF COLOR*

Just follow the Yellow Brick Road and you'll get to Emerald City! When environmental graphic design was an emerging discipline, the wayfinding strategy usually sold to hospitals was only slightly more sophisticated than the road so familiar to fans of *The Wizard of Oz*. In those days hospitals delineated colored paths on the floors of medical centers to define important routes around their facility. Just as the wizard proved to be unimpressive, the color-coded pathways proved inadequate over time, even misleading, as a solution to the daunting challenge of hospital wayfinding. To produce effective wayfinding solutions, designers must understand how to work with color on a case-by-case basis rather than relying on formulas. This chapter is not a primer about color theory or systems; it simply addresses essential information about using color as a wayfinding tool.

LEARN ABOUT
Using color as a powerful wayfinding tool

COLOR MEANING

Colors are a fundamental part of everyday life and greatly influence our experience of the world—it is almost impossible to imagine visual perception without them. Because people closely identify with colors, designers exploit them in powerful, evocative ways for all kinds of problem solving and often choose color as the central organizing element of a wayfinding design program. Colors can help people identify, navigate through, and even connect emotionally to a place. Although the latter idea seems abstract, it is important to realize that colors can mean different things to different people, depending on circumstances or demographics.

Nature is the source of some of our most primal relationships with color. Specific colors found throughout the natural world have obvious symbolic associations: bright red, the color of fire and lava, suggests heat, while a pure light blue, the color of ice or a clear sky, suggests cold. Although there are infinite variations and interpretations of red and blue, temperature is an obvious and universal association.

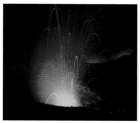 

Colors also signal cultural or patriotic nationalism. In the case of flags, minor layout variations can change what a color or color combination represents. The red, white, and blue of our Stars and Stripes symbolize the United States, for instance, but in the context of the Union Jack, these colors stand for the United Kingdom, our former ruler and now longtime ally. Depending on the flag layout, red and white can identify Canada, Switzerland, or Denmark. To make matters more complicated, minor layout modifications of the Swiss red cross on a white field turns it either into the flag of St. George, representing England, or a signal for the arrival of humanitarian and medical aid.

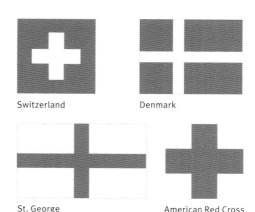

Switzerland   Denmark

St. George   American Red Cross

More recently, color has come to be associated closely with politics. In the past few election cycles, Americans have heard a lot about red states (Republican, mostly conservative) and blue (Democratic, mostly liberal). This color shorthand sums up political allegiances and rallies people, but it can also be divisive. Since the early twentieth century, red has denoted Communist affiliation. While an actual Green political party now exists, the term also stands for a global movement dedicated to environmental awareness and climate concern.

Color changes can also mark the passage of time. In the North American marketplace, greeting card publishers and retailers roll out a color calendar in sync with seasons and holidays such as Valentine's Day (red and pink), Easter (pastels), St. Patrick's Day (green), Halloween (black and orange), and Christmas (green and red). Lighting designers for the Empire State Building have taken this concept even further, into the urban sky. The landmark's elegant spire is an eye-catching beacon that glows with iconic colors to celebrate holidays and special events—everything from Gay Pride Day (lavender) to the New York Giants' spectacular 2008 Super Bowl victory (sapphire blue).

Colors became fundamental for wayfinding early in the twentieth century when American traffic engineers developed a standardized color-signal vocabulary to impose order on increasingly chaotic vehicular roadways. The basic palette, green (go), yellow (caution/yield), and red (stop), is now used around the world for traffic lights. Universally understood and applied, these color standards form the basis for the American traffic signage system, defined in the *Manual on Uniform Traffic Control Devices*, and influence safety by instantly conveying vital information to pedestrians and drivers alike.

COLOR TECHNOLOGY

While color meaning informs wayfinding, it is essential for designers to have a working knowledge of color mechanics beyond the basics. Everyone is familiar with the classic rainbow spectrum defined by Sir Isaac Newton—red, orange, yellow, green, blue, indigo, violet—and that pairs of primary colors (red, blue, and yellow) produce secondary colors (purple, green, and orange), while all three primaries together make black. In the case of projected rather than reflected light, the primary color palette changes to red, green, and blue. Overlapping these three primaries results in either natural or synthesized white light.

Colors are also distinguished by three properties: hue, intensity, and value. Hue refers to color variation, such as pure redness or greenness. Intensity is the saturation or density of a color. Value refers to its relative lightness or darkness. Understanding these properties enables the designer to control a palette for legibility and to project the desired meaning. For instance, when assembling an appropriate set of colors for coding purposes, it is helpful to pick colors of similar value so they fit together well as a set. Color intensity affects legibility: on a sign, contrasting intensities differentiate between the type and panel colors, as in any figure/field relationship. Hue selection usually

The Spectrum

In this color spectrum, the solid triangle points to the three primary colors, and the dashed one marks the secondary colors.

Color Values

The three colors of the top sign are of similar value and work well together as a color set. White type sits comfortably and legibly on all three. The bottom set of three is not as successful. First, the overlay type does not read equally well on all three colors; second, the darker top band dominates the panel design.

3.3

Contrast

These examples show the impact of color intensity on legibility and contrast. The most legible examples are those where there is more variation in the intensity of the two colors between text and background.

affects a design's overall appropriateness and meaning for a given context—it is important that a designer choose colors that best represent a building or site's function and context. A designer familiar with these will be able to fluidly manipulate color and achieve the preferred results.

As a practical matter, designers must be conversant with lighting technology, industry color standards, and computer software in order to identify, present, test, and specify exact colors for signage and other applications. The computer offers amazing ways to explore the riches of the spectrum, such as instant access to color swatch libraries and sophisticated color selection software. The Pantone Matching System (PMS) is the most pervasive and comprehensive tool for identifying colors on the computer, for print, and for other media. Most wayfinding designers are familiar with PMS numbers, organized by hue, value, and intensity. It is also possible to use the computer's color-spectrum window to choose special spot colors. These color selections can be further altered by tinting (digitally creating lighter shades or tones) or by changing proportions of CMYK (cyan, magenta, yellow, black) process colors.

COLOR SELECTION

How does a designer choose a single color when faced with all these choices? First, narrow down hue combinations that are appropriate for the architectural or environmental context. Next, consider two other important criteria: contrast and legibility, both essential for successful wayfinding. Generally signs must be highly visible to people approaching a site: the panels should be apparent from a distance, and the lettering and field must contrast sufficiently for the message to be read easily. Assuming a message's typographic treatment is sound, careful consideration of color combinations will ensure appropriate contrast and legibility. The Americans with Disabilities Act recommends that there be a 70 percent contrast between type and sign-panel backgrounds. Having developed conceptual designs, the designer moves to real space, creating mockups and color studies to check the color's functionality on site.

Light conditions have a major impact on color perception. What is the average day like at the project site? Is it the brilliant sunshine of the Southwest or the cloudy gray light of the rainy Northwest? The sunny haze of an August day in New York casts quite different light than the sunshine on a clear, crisp day in San Francisco. Artificial interior and nighttime illumination are additional light-source conditions to consider. Again, research and testing in actual or equivalent conditions is essential to assess how proposed colors will look and work. Material selection also comes into play, not only because surfaces have different reflection qualities, but also because certain lighting conditions can damage the colored surfaces of sign panels. Harsh bright sunlight with strong UV rays can cause certain colors, like red and black, to fade more quickly. An internally illuminated sign looks very different at night, with translucent glowing panels, than when it is reflecting light during the day.

Specifying color for fabrication purposes is not just about selecting paints or other substances to cover a surface: materials are often chosen for their own unique color and surface qualities. These days, with countless varieties of materials to choose from (see chapter 3.5),

Daytime and nightime views of an illuminated sign

the designer needs to understand the characteristics of different materials and surfaces, whether glass, plastic, metal, or recycled paper. All have specific color ranges, and often the richest color palette combines surface material and paint finishes in a distinctive way.

Once colors have been selected or created on the computer, it is necessary to specify them for actual application to signage. One method is to find a match using the PMS color swatch book. Another is to refer to commercial paint-matching systems like Benjamin Moore and Sherwin-Williams, large all-purpose paint companies with vast color libraries that are widely available. Matthews Paint Company, a division of PPG, and AkzoNobel are the paint manufacturers most commonly used for signage. The colors in each of these paint libraries are identified by a unique number system for specification purposes. There are also specialized paint systems such as DuPont's Imron line, which offers especially durable and glossy automotive-type paints for special outdoor applications.

The designer must guarantee that a color specified, presented, tested, and approved by the client will be the actual color that appears on final signs. To avoid any problems, it is essential to get chips and color samples from the sign fabricator to ensure a perfect match. These samples should then be archived to serve as color control during a wayfinding system's fabrication phase and, later, for maintenance purposes.

MATERIAL CONSIDERATIONS

Materials specified for signage vary enormously and offer limitless color effects. The choices are usually dictated by the setting. The natural colors of stone and wood have a fundamental integrity. Metals are among the most commonly specified materials and in their natural form fall into two broad families: white metals, including stainless steel, aluminum, and nickel; and yellow metals, such as brass and bronze. Finishing techniques for materials like anodizing aluminum broadens the color range even further. Manmade materials such as plastics offer unlimited color ranges (see chapter 3.5).

Painted wall in a medical center serves as area identification

Dramatically illuminated rods enliven a parking garage, transforming it into a civic landmark

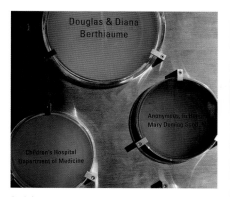

Inscribed lettering on a stone plaque at a university

Bronze plaque for theater interior

Stainless steel and glass Petri dishes with colored plastic inserts for research center donor signage

COLOR AS A WAYFINDING TOOL

Choosing the right colors for a wayfinding project results from knowing how to balance art and science. Art is the creative spark that inspires the designer to find interesting, comfortable, or surprising color combinations for memorable design solutions. Science ensures that those colors will physically work together for a particular project. For instance, a university wayfinding system often employs a cherished set of school colors, whereas practicality and safety dictate signage color for hospitals and subways. In retail design the sky's the limit—often the more colors, the better. Colors that make good sense in Miami Beach probably will not seem right in New York City. In reality there are no hard and fast rules, and the best designers break rules all the time.

Developing a complex wayfinding system is a collaborative process. As it usually involves many players and interests, it is best to steer the conversation away from matters of personal taste—"we like red"—to objective matters of color function. With experience, the designer learns how to work with clients to arrive at successful choices, explaining why color choices were made, how they work in their context, and the desired effect.

What are tangible uses of color for wayfinding? The most obvious, color coding, has advanced far beyond the Yellow Brick Road or those ineffective pathways on the hospital floor. Today most color-coding strategies either define distinct areas within a space or provide a basis for understanding the organization of a complex facility. The simplest wayfinding systems differentiate zones, such as the levels of a multistory parking garage, by using numbers, colors, and symbols. Other systems help people visualize how to navigate larger or more complicated spaces, such as urban districts or the buildings in a large medical center. For instance, Downtown Baltimore's pedestrian wayfinding system uses signs with colored panels to identify the seven districts of the downtown area. These signs reinforce the You Are Here quality of the system, helping visitors identify their location and sense the boundaries of a given neighborhood.

Signage for JFK International and Newark International airports

Downtown Baltimore

These color-coded district identification panels mark the seven areas of Downtown Baltimore. They are mounted adjacent to a main directional panel that guides people to destinations.

Color coding can also designate function. The signage system developed for the New York and New Jersey airports uses color fields to code messages in a different way, somewhat akin to highway signing. For example, yellow signs present directions related to air travel, terminals, gates, and baggage claim areas; green signs signal the way to ground transportation services like taxis, rental cars, and public transit; and black fields mark airport amenities, such as restrooms or information.

Color is not only a means to simplify users' perception of a place and provide prompts to guide them where they are going, but it can also breathe life into an otherwise purely utilitarian design. Today's digital-reproduction methods and sophisticated surface options offer unlimited choices; final color selection is ultimately up to each designer's best judgment. Although the range of colors available might seem daunting at first, be confident that careful planning and testing will help identify ones that are exactly right.

Sydney Exhibition and Convention Centre

Color is used to mark the numbered entrances of the Sydney Exhibition and Convention Centre. Large totems with numbered color beacons point the way to the different halls that make up the convention center.

COLOR AS IDENTITY

In addition to their usefulness for wayfinding, colors can also create a brand or identity. Signature colors create immediate associations for people and help build brand aware-ness and place recognition. Luxury retailers have understood this concept brilliantly. Tiffany, Hermès, and Fauchon, for example, have elevated fairly ordinary

colors—turquoise, orange, and pink—to mythic status by imbuing them with their brand's cachet. Color branding often proves useful for wayfinding in busy environments, and retail designers exploit color to differentiate brands or products, particularly in highly competitive arenas such as gas stations and car-rental companies. The latter has appropriated almost the entire color spectrum: red (Avis), yellow (Hertz), green (National), and blue (Thrifty). Lined up side by side at an airport, these easily distinguished colors help consumers identify the various rental counters quickly from long distances.

A strong color choice can also help create a signature identity for a public institution. The signs at Wave Hill, a small botanic garden in New York City, use a strong olive green for the sign panels. Set against the stone piers of the entry, these green signs signal arrival and make a statement about place. Located amidst the lush landscape of the gardens, the signs recede somewhat. The striking green ties the wayfinding system together and makes a coherent statement for visitors.

Wayfinding designers employ color in four ways. For complex environmental graphic systems, they may use several of these strategies in tandem. The most basic color application simply identifies a location or site by associating it with one or more specific hues. In some cases the colors support an existing corporate, institutional, or civic branding program. Colors can also subtly evoke a special sense of time and place, as at temporary events such as Olympic Games or large urban festivals. More technical applications of color, especially ones that code categories of information, are fundamental to effective wayfinding. For instance, without color coding it would be nearly impossible to differentiate transit lines, pedestrian pathways, or urban districts graphically on maps and signage. Finally, designers often choose colors purely for their inspirational qualities. Experiencing a color that fits perfectly with its context uplifts people and enhances their journey.

 ## The Color Expert

My work embraces the psychological aspect of color perception and how it affects consumer or user preferences. I glean information through word-association studies that reveal how people feel about colors and their emotional value—what draws their attention, what does not, and why.

As a part of my research, I show people samples of color families in order to gauge their reactions. We try to avoid drawing simplistic conclusions, such as red says this or blue says that. Statements along these lines are published all the time, which is ludicrous because colors can range from pastels to dark tones. What I've learned is that people feel an inherent sense of power when a color is darkened, making it seem more assertive and also more credible. The power of a particular shade of dark blue, whether it's used for signage or fashion, will bear more weight than a soft blue, gray blue, or mid-blue. People perceive navy blue differently from black, and although the colors seem very close, they still regard black as the most powerful color of all.

Popular reactions to colors evolve, and brown is a perfect example. At one time if you showed someone a sample chip of brown, you would inevitably hear "earthy" or "dirty." Today we have what I call the Starbucks Phenomenon: people now refer to brown as "rich," "robust," "aromatic," something to do with chocolate or coffee. Years ago orange was a hard sell in this country because it was always considered a downscale fast-food color. Vogue magazine recently showed a black Porsche helicopter with orange trim and a model with an orange ribbon wrapped around her, and Hermès has used orange for years. Yet I still hear people say that orange cheapens or declasses a design, and wonder what planet they're on.

Just as real estate is about location, location, location, color is all about context, context, context. Designers need to consider where a color will be used, what type of lighting is likely, and appropriate color mixtures. It very dangerous to make assumptions about a specific cultural or ethnic group's color preferences based on acknowledged precepts. When people move to a new country or culture, they often adapt in the way they perceive color. Their sensibilities depend on socioeconomic factors, their educational level, and how recently their family immigrated. Twice a year I meet with Italian, French, English, and Dutch citizens to discuss color trends. Although everyone comes from a different background, we're able to agree on a color forecast as if by osmosis because everyone is using the web for research and networking together, so there's a huge cultural crossover.

Design professionals also have to deal with clients with strong color preferences or aversions. The latter is one of the biggest problems I encounter—it means that the client honestly doesn't understand what the design is trying to accomplish. If you truly believe in your color choice for a design, then explaining it becomes one of your most important challenges.

Leatrice Eiseman heads the Eiseman Center for Color Information and Training and is executive director of the Pantone Color Institute.

OTHER VOICES: LEATRICE EISEMAN

3.4 SYMBOLS AND MAPS

*It is in terms of symbolic, concrete forms that the designer ultimately
realizes his perceptions and experiences, and it is in a world of symbols
that the average man lives. The symbol thus becomes a common language
between artist and spectator.*
PAUL RAND, *THOUGHTS ON DESIGN*

In most cases the primary conveyors of wayfinding information are the words we place on signs to identify destinations or to describe the path to a place. However, symbols and maps are powerful graphic tools that support the work done by those words. Symbols communicate visually rather than verbally and to people who may not speak the native language of a place. While wayfinding symbols deliver information at a glance, maps are more complex visual images that tell stories about a place. Maps provide specific orientation diagrams to explain public places to visitors, describe the arrangement of spaces, show where things are located, and help people orient themselves. They are essential for the wayfinding toolbox, primarily because they can say so much so concisely.

LEARN ABOUT
Graphics that support the verbal
messages on signs

THE POWER OF SYMBOLS

Wayfinding systems are often created for large, complex, and sometimes confusing environments. People may be coming from different places and headed in many directions, looking for multiple destinations. While hundreds of signs may be necessary to provide directions in such environments, a few well-chosen symbols can eliminate the unnecessary.

Symbols provide a shorthand pictorial representation of a place, a service, or an action. The man and woman icons for public bathrooms are probably the most pervasive public symbols. Regional, cultural, and artistic variations make for a wide spectrum of images for those icons, but the basic message is the same. For the purposes of this discussion, symbols refers to these iconic graphic devices. These are not to be confused with logos, which can often look like symbols but refer instead to business entities or organizations.

There are some classic examples of public places where symbols are essential and effective. In a large European train station, where people of many languages regularly pass through, symbols help guide people to the information booth or the food services. Symbols are used everywhere at the Olympics, directing people to different sport venues and to public services. In locations where visitors come from many countries or cultures, symbols are the common language that speaks to everyone. In a large teaching hospital in the United

States, symbols aid different groups of people: distressed English speakers, the increasingly diverse populations that inhabit American cities, and international customers who have traveled across the globe to get health care at these great institutions can all decipher the language of these symbols.

THE VOCABULARY OF WAYFINDING SYMBOLS

The most basic role of symbols is to identify services available in airports, train stations, shopping malls, office buildings, hospitals, and other public places where people gather. These symbols either accompany the verbal description of the service or stand alone to act as a beacon. In either case they strengthen communication.

The set of fifty pictograms developed by the AIGA, a leading professional design association, for the United States Department of Transportation (DOT) has become the standard symbol family for wayfinding purposes since its completion in 1981. Now nearly universal in public facilities here and abroad, they address everything from restrooms and escalators

AIGA/DOT symbols

to ferry terminals. The symbols mostly define places, like a stairwell or pharmacy, but also services, such as currency exchanges or a checked-baggage area. The set also includes some prohibitions like No Smoking. Since the debut of the AIGA/DOT symbols, several additional symbol sets have been created for areas of public

Recreation symbols

SYMBOLS FOR PLACEMAKING AND WAYFINDING

Symbols can also establish a sense of place while functioning as wayfinding tools. Here are some examples of pictograms that are unique to a particular location and communicate the qualities of that building or place.

assembly where good wayfinding is desirable. In 1991 the Society for Environmental Graphic Design (SEGD) created 108 new recreation symbols to complement the transportation symbols, and they are now in use at parks, greenways, and forest preserves.

Health-care symbols

Hospitals are notoriously complex environments; symbols can simplify communication with anxious visitors. Working under the sponsorship of the Robert Wood Johnson Foundation and in conjunction with partner Hablamos Juntos, SEGD led the development of a health-care symbol set in 2005. These symbols depict the various medical disciplines found in hospitals. The original intent of this project was to provide better access to health-care facilities for non-English speakers in the United States, but the net result may be better accessibility for all. Additionally, the SEGD created four symbols to help indicate the location of accessible facilities, as mandated by the Americans with Disabilities Act (ADA).

Accessibility symbols

Radio City Music Hall

Completely restored in 1999, Radio City's public spaces now reflect their original art deco grandeur. An original typeface design (see Other Voices, page 79), based on the lettering of a few extant signs from the 1930s, complements the period interiors. Accompanying illustrative symbols identify basic services and regulations.

MoMA QNS

During its Midtown renovation, the Museum of Modern Art (MoMA) relocated to an old factory in Queens. To establish a real presence there for this vibrant cultural venue, the museum adopted a striking moniker, MoMA QNS, plus a special typeface and symbol set. Together these defined a bold, alternative MoMA brand that informed the wayfinding program for the museum's temporary home.

Olympic Icons

The Olympics have become a tremendous opportunity for environmental graphic designers. Each Olympiad debuts a new symbol family and color palette, a graphic vocabulary, and a family of symbols for different sports that all add to the visual pageantry televised around the world. On site, colorful ephemera and environmental graphics heighten the spectator experience.

Munich 1972   Atlanta 1996   Sydney 2000   Beijing 2008

British Railroad Stations

A family of symbols reinforces the unique name and special historic character of the major British railroad stations. These symbols appear on signage, publications, and maps.

Victoria   King's Cross   Charing Cross   Gatwick Airport

Liverpool Street   Euston   Paddington   Manchester Piccadilly

Linimo Station Symbols

These symbols were created for the stations of Aichi Rapid Transit's Linimo line in Japan. The symbols are a distinctive set of marks that help travelers identify the different stations on the line.

PRINCIPLES OF MAP MAKING

While signs point the way to destinations and identify places, maps provide the best way to give visitors an overview of a public place. They depict the layout and organization of a complex, a building, or a space and show the relationships between the elements of a place and the pathways between. Using the You Are Here marker and the map key, people can situate themselves in a space and discover where things are located. While some of us love a good map, others are intimidated and put off by them. In order to be universally accessible, maps need to be simple and clear and present the appropriate information in the correct hierarchies.

One of the first questions is what area to include in the map. The zone of interest should be the focus of the map, with enough context to be useful but not distracting. Maps are usually presented with north at the top; however, sometimes it is expedient to shift the orientation a few degrees to allow a city or campus grid to be parallel to the sign borders. In either case it is important that people viewing an installed map face the same direction as that indicated by the map. If not, the map will be nearly useless as people will struggle to decide about going to the left or right.

The map's graphic language should be appropriate to the information requirements and the characteristics or geography of the setting depicted. Colors can be used at least three ways: to differentiate locations and features, such as roads, pathways, buildings, parks, and waterways; to code functional elements of the site, including zones, entryways, and floors; and to add style, personality, or character.

Maps can be labeled with text directly on the illustration or by means of a key. The key lists the different symbols, colors, and marks that appear and shows how to decode the information. A You Are Here designation is essential on a map to indicate the visitor's current location as well as those of other map installations. Listings of names often accompany the map of a campus, a city center, or shopping mall and can be organized alphabetically; numerically, by their reference numbers on the map; or by category. As information often needs to be updated, maps should be produced for easy alteration without having to change

or rebuild an entire kiosk sign. One way is to laminate a new digital printout each time corrections are necessary. Electronic displays allow for even easier updating.

These two campus maps show how the above principles are applied in practice.

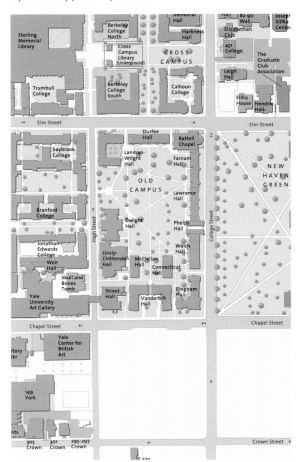

Yale University, New Haven, Connecticut

This plan view is a simple rendering of the historic Yale campus and presents the geography of the streets and buildings. The color palette is designed to give a readable,

balanced image of the campus and to differentiate buildings from streets, parks, and open spaces. Symbolic representations of trees give a sense of the foliage.

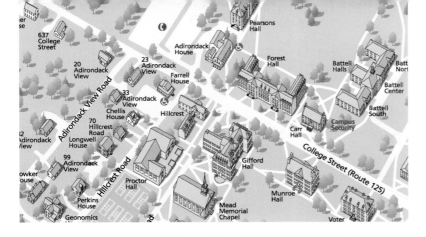

Labels on map:
637 College Street
20 Adirondack View
23 Adirondack View
33 Adirondack View
Adirondack House
Farrell House
Pearsons Hall
Forest Hall
Battell Halls
Battell North
Battell Center
Battell South
Chellis House
Hillcrest
70 Hillcrest Road
Longwell House
Adirondack View
99 Adirondack View
Campus Security
Carr Hall
Gifford Hall
College Street (Route 125)
Proctor Hall
Perkins House
Munroe Hall
Mead Memorial Chapel
Geonomics
Voter
Adirondack View Road
Hillcrest Road

Middlebury College, Middlebury, Vermont

This axonometric map's dimensional design captures the beauty of traditional stone buildings in the school's bucolic Vermont setting with naturalistic colors and trees located where they actually appear on the site. Intended for visitor wayfinding, the map appears both on printed guides and on campus-directory signs.

The Map Designers

As map designers for wayfinding systems, we have developed rigorous standards for informational hierarchy, typography, and color. Cartographers today focus mainly on database maps, which are often complex but visually unsophisticated because the original digital data they receive is crude or inadequate. Additionally, technical cartographic training rarely promotes understanding of, or commitment to, design quality. In a sense what we are doing is anachronistic: it integrates the design, illustration, art, and visualization skills once practiced by traditional map designers.

We formed our own design studio in order to concentrate on creating special-purpose maps and information graphics—that is, organizing complex information to make it accessible and comprehensible to the user. We have studied and practiced graphic design, architecture, and planning; and prior to establishing our practice, our work experience included positions at the Walker Art Center as well as at the offices of Charles and Ray Eames and, later, Saul Bass. Clients learned about us through word-of-mouth or by seeing our work on-site or on our website. Today we design two- and three-dimensional maps for facilities across the country, including airports, museums, zoos, parks, universities, and transit systems.

Before beginning a new project, we ask the client about the map's purpose, its audience, intended lifespan, and budget because our design decisions are based entirely on project requirements. We request comprehensive site documentation for reference, such as aerial and site photos, and a CAD base map, which we usually redraw to fulfill our needs. Our 3-D bird's-eye view maps—axonometric drawings of terrain, buildings (interior or exterior), and landscape—also begin with a high-quality plan drawing. Selecting the perfect angle of view is critical for this type of map, so we brief the client on various options. Sometimes, for clarity and ease of use, we distort or rotate the view so that north does not face up.

To map the Yale University campus, we received a CAD base drawing that served as a template over which we laid out a scaled plan drawing of all the roads, blocks, and pathways. The CAD map had been drawn from aerial photos and did not show the walkways between or through the buildings obscured by roofs. To make the walking paths and public areas more evident, we redrew the footprints of all the campus buildings from individual floor-plan drawings and pasted them onto our new base map at the correct scale and position. We concurrently worked on compatible color and typographic design in order to integrate all the graphic elements. After several rounds of tests and changes, we supervised the printing production in order to ensure the best possible reproduction quality for the maps that now appear in the university's outdoor display cases.

Jack and Gay Reineck are principals of Reineck & Reineck Design, a full-service information design firm specializing in custom maps, diagrams, and guidebooks.

Public Places

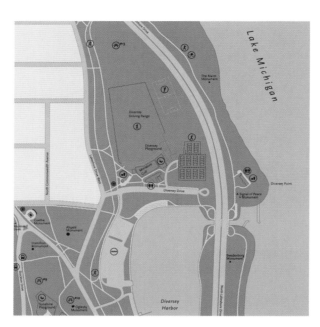

Lincoln Park, Chicago, Illinois

This map, created for a city-wide signage program, depicts just one section of the enormous 1,200-acre lakefront park. It details park geography, primary roads, pathways, and public facilities in relation to the immediate urban context, which is displayed as a grid of adjacent streets. The color palette and graphic language are deliberately simple, and symbols mark public services.

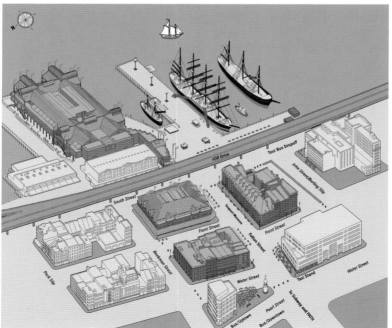

South Street Seaport, New York, New York

This three-dimensional map provides a pictorial view of the historic waterside district. The map provides a detailed axonometric illustration of the arrangement of the streets, the nineteenth-century historic buildings along the streetscape, and ships docked at the piers.

City Centers

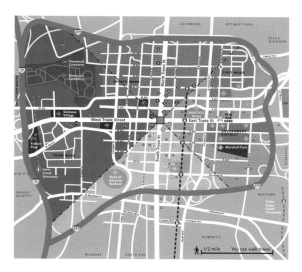

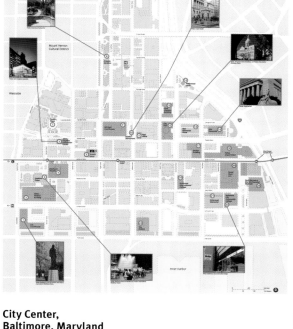

Uptown Charlotte, North Carolina

The map highlights what is locally known as Uptown, Charlotte's central district within the interstate loop. To help pedestrians and drivers orient themselves more easily, the area was divided into four zones, based on the cardinal points, that are color coded both on the map and on signage.

City Center, Baltimore, Maryland

This map for Baltimore's City Center district was created for a pedestrian wayfinding kiosk. Neighborhood bound-aries and buildings are defined in shades of green. A darker color sets off significant destinations, which are also identified with photographs.

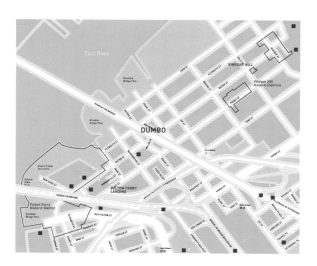

DUMBO/Fulton Landing, Brooklyn, New York

Created for the Downtown Brooklyn pedestrian way-finding system, this map's bold colors capture attention and support the brand iden-tity program for a rapidly developing neighborhood (see chapter 3.1, page 72). The map shows streets, parks, historic and retail districts, subway stops, and visitor destinations also fea-tured on directional signs.

Retail Complexes

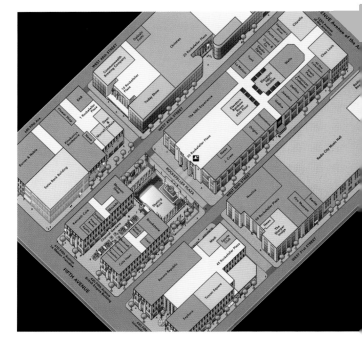

Rockefeller Center, New York, New York

This map shows the ground-floor retail areas of New York's famed Rockefeller Center. The axonometric drawings reflect the aesthetic of the landmark deco architecture and show the buildings' placement in the city grid. Colors define the different kinds of retail areas.

Grand Central Terminal, New York, New York

This "exploded" dimensional map pulls apart the three public layers of the terminal, suspending them in a stacked format to reveal the features of the station in their entirety. The map serves both as a directory for wayfinding and as a decorative graphic celebrating the landmark building's comprehensive renovation and expanded retail amenities with stylistic elements—illustrative logo, sculpture drawing, constellation imagery, and historic typeface—that recall its grand early-twentieth-century architectural legacy. Color coding of the plans and the accompanying listings facilitates visitor use of the retail-tenant directory.

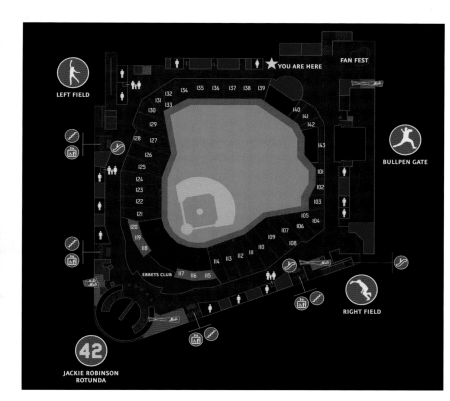

Specialized Interiors

Citi Field,
Queens, New York

Citi Field, the new home of the Mets, is a stadium complex with multiple entry points, different classes of seating, and many amenities. In this map highlighting the numbered general-seating areas, symbols and colors describe circulation and amenities. The entry/exit points of the field level are identified by playing field zones or ballpark landmarks, such as the Jackie Robinson Rotunda.

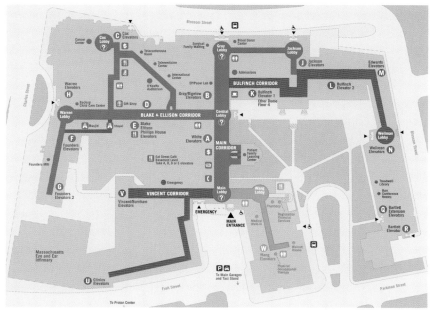

Massachusetts General Hospital,
Boston, Massachusetts

Because this map focuses on the wayfinding strategy for the entire complex, individual buildings are rendered as one continuous structure. It highlights the system of color-coded lobbies and corridors as the primary means of public navigation, and elevators are labeled with letters. These designations are reinforced on interior signs.

3.5 FORMS, MATERIALS, AND MEDIA

The time and place have to be right for the implementation of a new technology—but once the conditions are right, the technology can change our lives.
AMIR D. ACZEL, *THE RIDDLE OF THE COMPASS*

When young designers work on a wayfinding program for the first time, they often envision a few sign panels as an effective way to display useful information. Sometimes the best solution for a project is as simple as that. Usually, however, the creative challenge is far greater, and the rewards more satisfying for designer and client alike, when wayfinding moves beyond signage into the realm of full-fledged, multidimensional environmental graphic design. Learning to work effectively with forms, materials, and processes empowers the designer to imagine more inventive concepts and holistic solutions for the wayfinding problem at hand.

LEARN ABOUT
How to create three-dimensional forms and use materials, fabrication processes, and electronic media

THINKING BEYOND TWO DIMENSIONS

The wayfinding designer needs to appreciate that three-dimensional structure and detailing can impact the look of a system as much as color and typography. Great environmental graphic design meshes the communication designer's expertise with the problem-solving capabilities of industrial designers and architects who routinely think about objects and forms—from chairs and can openers to houses and great public buildings. Using sculptural forms to support information is a fascinating challenge, and done skillfully, it enriches wayfinding design.

Historically, signs were integral to the fabric of public architecture. Many early cultures, particularly Roman, mastered the art of incising inscriptions directly into stone facades and monuments. While carving letters by hand is still practiced, environmental graphic design encompasses a range of forms, media, materials, and processes previously unimaginable.

Wayfinding programs typically have signs that are either freestanding or attached to buildings and other structures. Grouped into a coherent system, these different types of signs can express the distinct character that establishes the identity of an entity or a place. At Mount Holyoke College, traditionally styled sign panels on dark metal posts suggest the school's heritage and prestige. In contrast, another venerable American academic institution, Massachusetts Institue of Technology, uses contemporary forms to project a very different image (left). In addition to

their obvious typographic and color differences, what really distinguishes these two sign programs are well-conceived forms, appropriate material selection, and careful detailing. Successful wayfinding designers must be adept at juggling all these variables and learn how to make a unique statement without overdesigning.

RELATING DESIGN IDEAS TO CONTEXT

While it is fairly straight-forward to describe the steps in the design-exploration process, explaining where inspiration for good three-dimensional design comes from is far more elusive. The designer's experience and sensibility drive this creative process. Most successful designers have a head full of ideas ready for the taking: these ideas come from the world at large, from visual references, from past projects, and from the situation at hand. Sometimes designers create image boards to show sources of inspiration and spark dialogue about design possibilities. Alternatively, the designer may jump right into the sketch process.

Before turning to an abstract concept, the designer should consider obvious contextual ideas such as the client's area of focus or geographic location. The fastening method used for a sign system at Children's Hospital Boston, for instance, recalls Tinkertoys. Aluminum rods and resin beads embellishing this flag sign make a colorful visual reference to childhood play. In the case of KeySpan Park, a minor-league baseball park in Brooklyn, stadium signs evoke sport by using a baseball motif to identify the box-office window.

In other cases an abstract design may be best when a more literal reference seems inappropriate or too difficult to illustrate. A simple graphic device, cleverly applied, may be all that is necessary to make a way-

Beacon Court identification pylon

Children's Hospital Boston
flag sign

Atlanta Federal Center room
identification sign

KeySpan Park box office sign

finding program distinctive. The wayfinding program for the Atlanta Federal Center uses a simple T-shaped device to separate the building number from the center's initials in one corner of the sign. This T-form also runs along the top of the sign as a rail for the required identification of the room in Braille. Sometimes an abstract form simply feels right for the setting and looks artful. A giant, slim pylon in New York's Midtown serves as a monumental marker sign for the entry to Beacon Court and accentuates the bold geometry of this urban public space.

THE PROCESS OF FORM EXPLORATION

Designing a wayfinding system entails making decisions about signs' key formal elements—shape, materials, and construction—while taking into account their setting, design intent, message, and audience. During this exploration, the designer first develops elements separately, then brings them together into a unified vocabulary. One way to begin is to create diagrams of the various categories of signs (see chapter 2.3) to understand the range of designs this specific project will require. These simple boxlike diagrams allow the designer and client to decide how various messages will be deployed in a space and how the wayfinding system functions as a whole.

If a project is complex and requires a large group of sign types, it is easy to become overwhelmed by all the variables—experienced designers just isolate two or three key sign types for initial study. This makes development manageable and allows the designer to consider a broad range of ideas in a short time. After the best approach is established, it can be extrapolated to the other signs. Rough, freehand sketches provide a useful way to study different forms quickly.

Once the preliminary designs are resolved, computer studies offer the most efficient way to render ideas more clearly for presentation purposes because they help designers synthesize forms, shapes, scale, typography, and colors into realistic images of actual signs. Some experienced designers prefer to show the client just one resolved idea, making the pitch that it represents the right approach. Others show two or three variations, encouraging a dialogue about each solution's merits. As the options are narrowed down and consensus builds around one approach, the designer then adds more detail to illustrate the sign's three-dimensionality. Simple section drawings with basic dimensions indicate the sign's scale and shape. Notations about materials and construction methods should be cited as well.

3.5

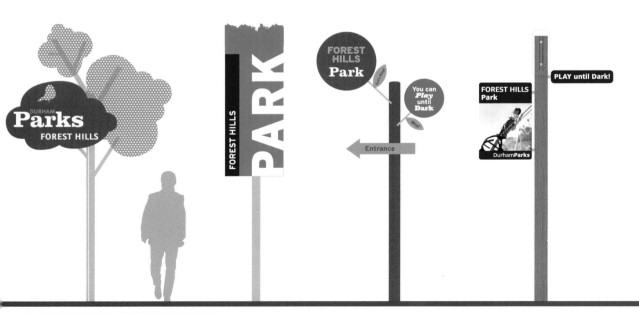

Four schematic designs for the same sign type

WHERE SIGNS ARE LOCATED

Understanding the spaces to be signed and the
sequence of messages they will communicate
guides the designer in deciding where and how to
mount signs in the system. Here are four examples
of different positions and mounting options.

Flag-mounted Signs

Located above head levels,
these signs, which resemble
flags, are useful in large open
halls and in busy corridors
where panels perpendicular
to the wall offer maximum
visibility. Symbol signs are
often mounted this way to
give quick nonverbal cues
about essential services, such
as gate numbers in public-
transportation facilities.

Wall-mounted Signs

These are generally smaller-
scale signs that identify
places, provide directions,
or state regulations. Most
interior signage, particularly
room identification signs, are
wall mounted. Exterior wall-
mounted signs either appear
low for pedestrian viewing
or higher to be seen from a
vehicle.

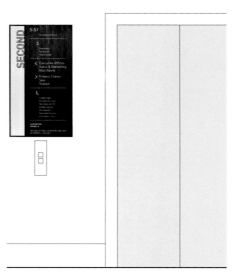

CREATING A FAMILY OF SIGNS

As the designer explores ideas, making decisions about
materials and details along the way, the sign family—
all the signs and other wayfinding elements necessary
for a specific project—comes together. In a wayfinding
system, all the signs usually share a common graphic
and formal language, as shown by these signs for an
urban park system.

SENATE CORRIDOR	MARYLAND CORRIDOR	CHESAPEAKE CORRIDOR
↑ Information Center **Ticket Office** **Security Offices** ♿	↑ **Halls A–E** **Wabash Ballroom** Rooms 101–110, 120–124	↗ **500 Ballroom & Reception** **Up to** Sagamore Ballroom Rooms 111–117
🚻 🍴	🚻 🍴 $	🚻 C

Ceiling-mounted Signs

This is the typical mounting method for large-scale over-head directional signs. These signs hang down from the ceiling, providing directions to major destinations in a public facility. It is important to consider their clearance and the lighting conditions to ensure that they fit comfortably in the space and that their messages will be legible.

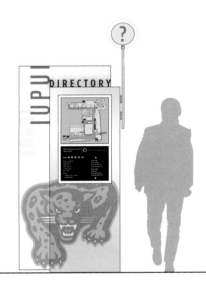

Freestanding Signs

There are innumerable styles of freestanding signs for both interior and exterior use. These may be single- or double-post assemblies, pylons and kiosks, or monument signs. Exterior freestanding signs can be scaled for either pedestrian or vehicular viewing.

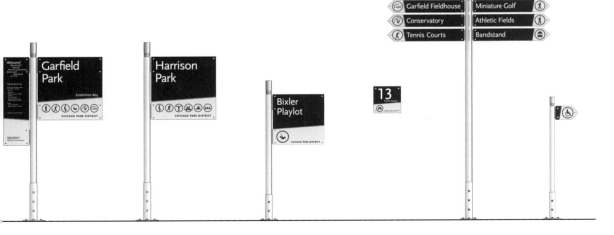

THE DEVIL IS IN THE DETAILS

After the designer sources, explores, and develops ideas, he or she refines and fleshes out the details. This is an iterative process that involves constant research, study, and review. The designer explores the best materials for the system and determines how the pieces should fit together: what type of material and finish the signs need; how they will be affixed to a building or mounted in the ground. The illustrations on pages 110–11 and charts on pages 114–17 provide an overview of some of the options available to the signage designer.

During the concept exploration, the designer consults with technical experts, such as lighting designers or structural engineers, who have specific expertise that will inform the process. Manufacturers' representatives and materials suppliers also provide information about products and processes, and capable fabricators are another great resource for the designer at this stage because they offer a wealth of knowledge about production and installation.

This exploded diagram of a post-and-panel assembly, for a freestanding bus-stop sign that displays several types of information, illustrates the level of detail the designer must resolve before a sign can be built. The drawing shows how various parts fit together and what hardware is necessary to connect them. The quality of the final sign depends upon the careful resolution of these details. For sign systems where these visible connections are part of the design statement, it is appropriate to reveal the hardware; in other cases the design may conceal all connections to create a more seamless graphic image.

Reduced-scale models showing massing and full-size mock-ups are essential for testing a sign concept. The mock-up provides an opportunity to check actual sizes of individual elements close-up and see how the structure feels in a space. It can also help client and designer determine whether the sign is the right scale and proportion, its panels are the appropriate size and thickness, and its typography is legible.

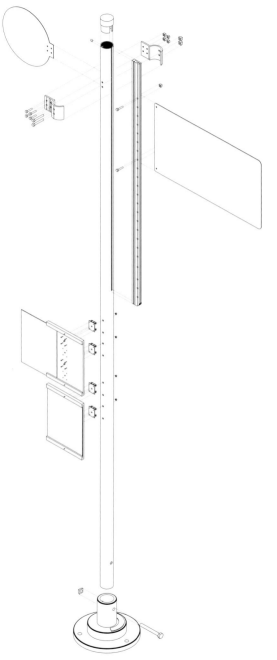

Exploded diagram of a typical post-and-panel sign

STOCK SIGN SYSTEMS

While many wayfinding systems have a custom design, there are times when it is appropriate to specify an off-the-shelf, or stock, sign system, from the many excellent options available. These are most useful for interior applications and for volume application, as in a hospital. Each manufacturer has its own standard back plate and sign panel and hardware system, and these systems usually allow some level of customization to give them a unique appearance.

The Architect

Our firm usually designs structures from the ground up, and I'm a big proponent of establishing a close collaboration with an environmental graphic design consultant early on to ensure that signage can be fully integrated into the architecture. This integration may be conceptual, to support the larger design aesthetic, or quite literal, physically incorporating signage into the bricks and mortar of the building itself.

Successful wayfinding projects don't challenge predictable human behavior. If an institution refers to a building by a specific name, then continue to use it. Don't fight the obvious. For instance, we designed a new building for the S. I. Newhouse School of Public Communications at Syracuse University. The goal of the school's administration was to unify this complex, so we didn't challenge the existing lingua franca that everyone uses. The three buildings in the school's complex all share one name, and we retained the nomenclature, identifying them as Newhouse 1, 2, and 3.

We were also asked to display the First Amendment on the exterior of Newhouse 3. While the design intent was to convey the permanence of the school's identity and respect the gravitas of the text, the inscription also needed to appear ephemeral and light enough to connote contemporary digital communications. To achieve this we used a special lamination technology that embeds the inscription in the glass of a clerestory window running the length of the building. Outside, people see the First Amendment emblazoned across the facade, and, depending on atmospheric conditions, the text appears to fade in and out. Inside, the text is invisible, thereby avoiding loss of daylight, backward lettering, or an obstructed view. As there wasn't enough real estate to display the entire passage, we evoked a kinetic "ticker" by breaking the text into phrases divided by architectural columns. All these elements reverberate, so the graphics and architecture play off each other very nicely.

Environmental graphic designers should avoid turning signage into a form of appliqué. Hiring a wayfinding design team after a building is complete does everyone a disservice. Though some environmental graphic designers may be willing to be called in late, apply what's needed, and just glue it on, more professional designers relish the opportunity to think about how to embed their work in the DNA of the architecture, and that's essential.

Tomas J. Rossant, AIA, is a partner in Polshek Partnership Architects.

OTHER VOICES: TOMAS J. ROSSANT, AIA

An Overview of Materials

The Basics

METALS

Metals are the most common sign material. Flexible and durable, they can be used for structural framing and visible surfaces, and dimensional elements. Typical signage metals vary in color from silver to yellow and come in a range of finishes, from polished to brushed or satin. Graphics can be etched, carved, painted or enameled, or applied.

GLASS

Glass is increasingly common for interior and exterior signage and can be backlit, edge lit, or made into dimensional forms. Painting, etching, carving, and sandblasting are the most common ways to treat surfaces; applying graphics and textures to either the front or back surface or an inner layer will change the effect of the sign.

WOOD

Wood is less durable for signage than other materials and can darken with time, whether for interior or exterior use. Letters and graphics are typically applied or etched. Wood can also be used for surface detailing or lamination on top of a background material. Sustainable sources should be considered.

STONE

Stone can be used for sign panels or bases, providing stability and integration with landscapes or architectural settings. Graphics and letterforms can be stud mounted to the face of the stone or incised into stone surface by carving or sandblasting. Letters can also be created with water-jet cutting.

Aluminum: the workhorse metal of the signage industry, all purpose; can appear in its natural state or be coated by anodizing or painting; cool gray color; low cost; highly recyclable; lightweight; strong resistance to corrosion

Stainless steel: can provide a sophisticated architectural image; versatile material; warm gray color due to nickel content; high cost; highly recyclable; extremely durable; heavyweight; stain, rust, and corrosion resistant

Bronze: primarily copper-tin alloy, offers low-key, historic flavor; signs can be fabricated from solid material or cast; dark yellow color; high cost; recyclable; malleable; durable; heavyweight; low resistance to corrosion and oxidation

Brass (also Muntz metal): primarily an alloy of copper and zinc; bright metal that can add sparkle to signage features, yellow color; moderate cost; recyclable; malleable; durable; medium weight; low resistance to corrosion and oxidation

Float: standard uniform, flat glass; greenish color; low-to-moderate strength; good durability; low cost; recyclable

Low-emissivity: glass with micro thin coating to reduce heat gain; clear white color; high strength; high durability; can be tempered and laminated; high cost; recyclable

Borosilicate: constituent elements help resist thermal shock; fair-to-high strength; high durability; can be tempered and laminated; high cost; recyclable

Fritted: ceramic patterns baked onto surface; high strength; high durability; can be tempered and laminated; moderate-to-high cost; recyclable

Tempered: safety glass; high strength; high durability; low-to-moderate cost; processed by thermal or chemical treatments; will shatter into cubed fragments upon impact

Laminated: safety glass; fair-to-high strength; high durability; low-to-moderate cost; will hold together when shattered; patterns or graphics can be applied to interlayers.

Oak: light tan with yellowish tint; hardwood; excellent durability; good finishing qualities; good workability; moderate price

Cedar: mix of cream and dark red; softwood; fair durability; good finishing qualities; fair-to-good workability; inexpensive

Pine: light yellow to yellowish brown; softwood; fair to good durability; fair finishing qualities; fair-to-good workability; inexpensive

Mahogany: reddish brown to medium red; hardwood; very good durability; excellent finishing qualities; excellent workability; expensive

Cherry: light brown to dark red; hardwood; excellent durability; excellent finishing qualities; good workability; moderate price

Poplar: creamy white to yellowish green; excellent stability and durability; ideal for sign frames; inexpensive

Granite: pink to dark gray/black; distinct graining, excellent durability; good workability; high cost

Limestone: usually gray, but also found in a range of yellows to pinks; excellent durability; good workability; moderate-to-high cost

Marble: great range of colors, purest being white; wide range of graining and textures; excellent durability; good workability; moderate-to-high cost

Sandstone: color varies; fair to good durability; good workability; high cost

Slate: gray to black, with notable directional graining; excellent durability; low-to-moderate cost

Synthetics

BANNERS

Banners are made of fabric, plastic, or other nonrigid materials and often require mounting structures on both top and bottom. Banners may be digitally printed, silk-screened, or decorated with appliquéd graphics. Often used in temporary exhibits, they can also be used outdoors if the material is durable and light-fast.

PLASTIC

Plastics represent a broad category of synthetic materials. For signage they are typically cut from cast or extruded sheets of varying thickness. Sheets can be colored or tinted and often add translucent properties to illuminated signage. Graphics can be painted, printed, or silk-screened. Plastic is a key component of stock or modular sign systems.

COMPOSITES

This category contains a broad range of engineered materials made of two or more parts with different physical or chemical properties. They can be used in many areas of signage from back plates to sign faces and can usually be cut into shapes and forms. With a range of textures and colors, composite materials can be painted or surface printed or used naturally.

Sustainable

GREEN/RECYCLED

"Green" materials not only have recycled content but also take into account manufacture, its by-products, modularity, and life span or ease of disassembly for recycling. Many manufacturers now follow LEED standards when developing new products; use of these materials can contribute towards LEED credits (see pages 122–23).

Vinyl: polyvinyl chloride (PVC) fabric; gloss finish; interior and exterior use; high durability; moderate cost; off-gassing occurs because of PVC

Nylon: synthetic, easily cleaned fabric; satin finish; interior use; moderate durability; lightweight; low cost; nonrecyclable

Tyvek: trademarked synthetic fabric; interior and exterior use; high durability and weather resistant; high cost; recyclable; manufacture is energy efficient

Poplin: woven cotton and/or polyester; matte finish; interior use; high durability; machine washable; moderate cost; woven cotton and/or polyester

Dacron: trademarked fine weave polyester fabric; interior and exterior use; high durability; high cost; nonrecyclable

Acrylic: interior and exterior use; moderate durability; low cost; excellent machinability; clear, translucent, or opaque

Lexan: a trademarked polycarbonate for interior and exterior use; high durability; excellent machinability; moderate cost

Cast resin: interior and exterior use; high durability; expensive cost; recyclable

Sintra: lightweight, rigid PVC foamboard with low-gloss finish; interior and exterior use; moderate durability; low cost; recyclable

Photopolymer: plastic with photosensitive coating that can be photo etched to create tactile graphics; useful for ADA-mandated raised text and Braille; interior and exterior use; high durability; low-to-moderate cost; nonrecyclable

Phenolic resin laminates: heat-pressed sandwich of digital print, melamine, and phenolic resin sheets; great application for changeable outdoor graphics and maps; interior and exterior use; high durability; high cost; nonrecyclable

Alucobond: sandwiched material of two sheets of aluminum over a plastic core, can be used as flat cut sheets or bent to create curved forms; interior and exterior use; high durability; expensive; partly recyclable

Fiberglass: glass fiber–reinforced polyester; can be used in sheets or molded, interior and exterior use; high durability; moderate cost

3form Ecoresin: 40 percent recycled resin; recyclable at end of life cycle; available in many colors, also has embedded patterns and graphics; currently for interior use only, exterior usage available in near future; accepts direct printing for text and graphics

Paperstone: 100 percent post-consumer-waste compressed paper using a nontoxic adhesive or binder; minimal energy used for material manufacture; accepts direct printing or engraving

EverGreen fabrics: PVC free; minimal energy use and no volatile organic compounds (VOC) emissions during material manufacture; interior and exterior grades; accepts digital printing

Lightblocks: translucent sustainable resin sheet material; wide range of colors; recyclable

Alkemi: recycled composite aluminum; strong and durable; available in multiple colors

Plyboo: natural material; rap-idly renewable; no VOC gas, nontoxic

An Overview of Fabrication Processes

Forms

CUTTING

Material cutting is necessary for all signage fabrication. Fabricating panels, custom shapes, dimensional letters, and custom-mounted pieces often begins with cutting. Most materials are machine cut, usually based on a digital template.

CREATING FORMS

Three-dimensional letters and symbols are often used as signs. The methods below can be integrated with other design processes described in this chart.

Graphics

ETCHING

Etching is a common way to create graphics and messages. Etching into a material's surface creates a recessed graphic while maintaining the original background finish. Reverse etching creates raised graphics by removing layers from the background. Graphics and letters are often filled with paint to increase contrast and legibility.

PRINTING

Printing applies text, images, and graphics onto a substrate. Colors are only restricted by the method chosen. Typical methods listed below can be used separately, as well as in combination on a single substrate.

Laser cut: a high-power laser aimed at the material cuts it either by melting, burning, or vaporizing; cut edges have a high-quality finish

Water-jet cut: a high-pressure stream of water plus an abrasive, cuts stone and metal up to 2 inches thick; also called hydrocutting

Router cut: rotating cutter shapes complex face and edge detailing, typically used with metal, wood, and stone

Die cut: a manufactured steel-die presses and cuts out a particular shape; commonly used for custom shapes and unique forms; also refers to the final cut object

Casting: a method for the mass production of solid metal or plastic letters, also used for specialty individual dimensional metal signs. Molten material is poured into a mold, typically made of rubber, metal, or sand. Once the cast material has cooled, it is removed from the mold and finished by hand. This method can be used to create acrylic forms with embedded light-emitting diodes (LED).

Fabricating: a dimensional letter, numeral, or other form, usually fabricated from thin metal or acrylic, joined, and soldered to appear solid. Also called a channel letter, it can contain internal lighting components for a face-lit, edge-lit, or rear-lit (halo) effect. Translucent faces, or sides, can have a film or vinyl applied to produce a colored light.

Acid etched: a stencil is applied to a metal or glass substrate by screen printing or a photopolymer process. The sign is dipped into or brushed with an acid mixture; primarily for marking glass. The surface is later washed and the stencil removed.

Photo etched: photo printing of a film image on a presensitized zinc plate, which is then processed and chemically etched to give a relief image

Engraving: a method of marking metal, plastic, or glass in shallow, negative relief utilizing an engraving bit

Sandblasted: a rubberized stencil applied to a glass, metal, or wood surface is sprayed with a pressurized stream of sand or synthetic particles until the desired depth is achieved

Carved: used for marking wood or stone; classic V-shaped letters or square-edged carvings are hand cut with chisel and mallet, sandblasted, routed, or engraved

Silk screen: using a squeegee, colored ink is pressed through stenciled or emulsified fabric stretched over a frame to print an image on fabrics or sign panels.

Vinyl appliqué: a digital printer cuts text or graphics from adhesive vinyl, which is then pressed into position on a substrate. Available in numerous opaque, translucent, metallic, and transparent colors.

Digital printing: large-format digital printers print images directly onto vinyl, fabric, or other roll-fed materials that can be used as banners or adhered to rigid back plates. Newer flatbed digital printers can print directly on rigid materials.

Mountings

ATTACHMENTS

Attachments are the hardware used to affix signs to a structure. Attachment methods have to be engineered both for safety and to fulfill aesthetic criteria. The design of attachments requires a knowledge of engineering, an understanding of field conditions, and a vision for the visual impact desired.

FOOTERS

Exterior signage requires secure ground attachments. A freestanding sign is anchored by a concrete footer or foundation. The footer stabilizes the sign against forces that may cause it to torque or fail and can be poured to be below grade (invisible) or above grade (visible) based on the design intent.

Surfaces

FINISHES

Finishing determines the final look, color, pattern, and quality for all visible aspects of a sign. A finish can be either a simple surface treatment or a covering for the material and is the best way to give a sign system visual unity. Finishes should also be considered for their green properties.

Mechanical fastening: prefabricated or custom detailed; typically nuts and bolts that hold a sign together

Blind fastening: mechanical attachments hidden from view for a seamless sign face; vandal resistant, tamperproof, removable, or permanent; also called concealed fastening

Pin mounting: a threaded rod, drilled and tapped into the back of a sign panel or dimensional letter, then inserted into a hole on the mounting surface and secured with a high-bond adhesive

Very high-bond tape (VHB): tape produced by 3M used for mounting sign panels to walls or graphics to sign panels. VHB eliminates mechanical fasteners or welded attachments and can be removed without damaging walls and foundations. Available in many grades and thicknesses.

Direct embed into footer: a direct embedding of the sign post into a poured footer; the post is braced to true vertical while the concrete cures.

Adhesive anchors into sidewalk: a mechanical anchor system adhered to a hollow vaulted sidewalk with a high-bond chemical agent. Anchors are mechanically fastened to a welded plate at the bottom of the post.

Break-away foundation: a separate post attachment, above grade, mounted to the foundation/footer; allows for ease of changing a damaged sign

J-bolts into footer: threaded J-bolt rods are permanently set into concrete footer/ foundation. A welded post/ baseplate is positioned over the rods and mechanically fastened.

Tube sleeve: combination attachment method utilizing a rod or tube extending from the concrete footer over which the hollow sign posts are inserted and mechanically fastened.

Clear coat: an extremely durable, clear lacquer finish; in descending order of reflectance: gloss, semigloss, 20 percent gloss (preferred by the ADA), eggshell, and matte or dead flat finish

Powder coating: a paint finish made from finely ground solid resins, usually applied electrostatically and then heat cured; very tough, flexible, and much harder to chip, crack, or peel than other coatings

Baked enamel: special enamel paint is sprayed or screenprinted on a metal surface, dried, and then cured with heat, resulting in a durable surface

Porcelain enamel: powdered glass and pigment is sprayed or screen-printed on a metal surface, then fired at a very high temperature, resulting in an extremely durable surface similar to some household appliances, with a long lifespan

Anodizing: an electrochemical coating applied to metal to harden, protect, and enhance its appearance, durability, and corrosion resistance. Typically applied to aluminum, it may tint or color the surface.

Oxidizing: metal surface combines with oxygen to make an oxide. Oxidized metal looks weathered or rusted; should be clear coated to maintain degree of oxidization

Chrome plating: an electrochemical process to plate steel, brass, or aluminum with chrome to create a mirror finish. Nickel plating is a similar process using nickel to create the mirror finish surface.

Brushed metal: a nonreflective, textured finish created mechanically or chemically for decorative purposes. Grained effect is usually created using sandpaper: long-grain finish is created by hand or via belt sander; short grain finish by an orbital sander.

Flame polish: a method of polishing a material, usually thermoplastics or glass, by exposing it to a flame or heat. As the material melts, surface tension smoothes out the surface. Done properly, flame polishing produces the clearest finish, especially for acrylic surfaces.

ELECTRONIC MEDIA

Fixed, static signs that guide people through and around spaces form the basis of most wayfinding systems. Increasingly, however, electronic and dynamic media are becoming valuable additions to the wayfinding tool kit. Because these media technologies are subject to constant change, it is helpful to break them down into several categories to understand their usefulness.

Large-Scale LED Displays

Art and advertising design have now morphed into a version of building signage and wayfinding. Large-scale dynamic LED image displays developed for urban outdoor advertising, and popularized by artist Jenny Holzer's gallery and museum installations, have become highly visible elements in many building signage programs, particularly those for large outdoor retail centers and sports stadiums. Technological advances continue to allow these displays to grow in size and improve in image resolution. Today, they take many forms: large-scale identification signs, advertising displays, exhibit environments, and image walls that wrap entire buildings. These signs are usually LED based and provide amazing opportunities to entertain, inform, and display branded content. When created to promote sponsor relationships, these large displays can generate huge revenues for building owners. Ultimately, their quality depends on the content. A client must face the ongoing challenge and expense of keeping images fresh, but handled expertly, the results can be spectacular.

Broadcast Monitors

Monitors represent a more conventional use of digital media. Traditionally the most pervasive use of these changeable displays has been in airports and other transportation facilities where video monitors provide essential information. Now this travel information is more commonly displayed on higher resolution LCD monitors or large-scale LED display boards. The designer's challenge is to apply good typographic principles to these broadcast displays. Beyond the world of transportation, these broadcast monitors now appear in any number of public places—hospitals, convention centers, hotels, universities, retail centers. In these environments, the content usually includes event listings, advertising or sponsorship, or a televised news feed. Unless their content is vital to the experience of a place, these displays can be distracting and not very informative.

Interactive Kiosks

Interactive kiosks are everywhere: most people already do the bulk of their banking at an ATM. The quality of the user-interface display can vary widely, but interactive kiosks are usually reliable and easily understood. Although this technology has been available for several decades, designers are still seeking the best and most appropriate ways to use it for wayfinding application. As at airports, hospitals are now using these kiosks to provide wayfinding information alongside the registration functions. Kiosks represent an exciting opportunity to communicate with diverse communities in multiple languages by providing tailored wayfinding instructions. The quality of this experience depends on an intuitive, well-scripted, and well-designed interface and durable functional hardware.

Mobile Wayfinding Devices

Because of the evolution of hardware, the increasing use of global positioning systems (GPS), and the growth of wireless networks, the mobile wayfinding device is one of the field's most rapidly evolving new territories. As wireless technology becomes more widespread and as personal digital assistants (PDAs) and cell phones offer even greater connectivity to the internet or other broadcast media, personalized wayfinding options will undoubtedly grow exponentially. Institutions are constantly exploring new uses of podcast downloads and other technologies to replace the traditional audio guide systems provided by museums to explain exhibitions. These all have applications for wayfinding. As demand for and quality of handheld devices grows

and their user interfaces improve, the use of fixed signs in complex environments may evolve. The design challenge is to create simplified displays that can be read and understood on small-scale display monitors. As people increasingly use mobile phone technology to build community and create connectivity, reliance on it for wayfinding purposes is sure to grow.

The World Wide Web

The World Wide Web has become the global digital resource for just about everything, from dating and networking to browsing and shopping. The web is the best research tool ever available for accessing up-to-the-minute news and information. People look up websites to plan trips, make reservations for events, and set up appointments. MapQuest paved the way, providing instant access to directions to any unfamiliar location. The range of data and images on Google Earth has greatly expanded our ability to virtually explore unfamiliar places both local and remote. As people come to rely on the web more and more for trip planning, it is important to connect the web-based information graphics and wayfinding terminology to the actual signage on site. This way, visitors will have a consistent experience of a place from the planning stage to arrival at the destination. As the web and on-site experiences merge and overlap, the roles of information architects and wayfinding designers blur and overlap.

The technological options described above present challenges for the wayfinding designer: when is it appropriate to use new media, and how should it be integrated into conventional signage? The designer can only answer these questions after conducting a thoughtful information-planning phase that considers a project's design goals as well as its communications requirements, spatial constraints, and budget. Assembling the right team is also important: successful electronic media design is a collaborative venture that brings together information planners, wayfinding designers, architects, hardware providers, and content developers. Though these new tools are remarkable and their electronic effects often dazzling, it is important to remember that their purpose is to serve design, not vice versa.

3.6 GREEN DESIGN FOR SUSTAINABILITY

We must choose instead to make the 21st century a time of renewal.
By seizing the opportunity that is bound up in this crisis, we can unleash the
creativity, innovation, and inspiration that are just as much a part of our
human birthright as our vulnerability to greed and pettiness.
The choice is ours. The responsibility is ours. The future is ours.
AL GORE, *AN INCONVENIENT TRUTH*

The design community across the country is rapidly adopting the principles of sustainable or "green" design intended to improve everyone's quality of life. Whether this is due to the high-profile accomplishments of individuals like the architect William McDonough, professional initiatives such as the Green Building Council's Leadership in Energy and Environmental Design (LEED) certification program, or simply a critical mass of public awareness given a significant boost by the Oscar- and Nobel-prize-winning efforts of Al Gore, understanding the environmental impact of one's work is now essential for designers and clients alike.

LEARN ABOUT
Incorporating sustainable solutions
into your design process

BECOMING FAMILIAR WITH GREEN DESIGN

Designers who develop a deep appreciation for sustainability's value do so by practicing it everyday at home and at work. Companies can introduce the concept of sustainability by showing staff how to be more environmentally responsible in their own workplace. Even earlier, design schools can expose students to similar ideas by incorporating sustainable principles into their curriculum. Regardless of their level of professional experience, designers who are personally familiar with sustainability have more incentive and insight to make sensible green choices for their projects (See Other Voices, page 125).

Designers also need to understand the terminology that applies to sustainability. While the terms *sustainable* and *green* are used interchangeably here to describe environmentally responsible products and practices, the World Commission on Environment and Development, also known as the Brundtland Commission, defines sustainability as a "way to satisfy present demands without compromising the ability of future generations to meet their own needs." While the commission's concept embraces a vocabulary of ideas and practices too voluminous to cover here, it nonetheless provides a lens through which the environmental graphic designer can view the creative process and learn how to make greener choices. Building on the LEED rating system, a set of standards for incorporating environmentally sustainable design and construction principles in building projects, the SEGD's Green Committee published its first Green Paper outlining a framework for these choices in 2007.

The fundamental goal of a green environmental graphic design (EGD) process is to design for the lifespan of the project. This key determination is the framework for the following four strategies, which may be incorporated, all or individually, into any project:

1. Air quality and environmental impact

Consider how to reduce or eliminate waste and pollutants that are the by-products of manufacturing, fabrication, and installation processes.

2. Waste management and disposability

Understand how any such by-products (and others, such as packing material) and the object itself may be disposed of when no longer useful for the original purpose.

3. Recyclability

Select materials that can be converted easily ("upcycled" or "downcycled") for another use at the end of their life span.

4. Energy and lighting efficiency

Consider how energy can be used most efficiently throughout the project—in manufacturing, transportation, and illumination of the final products—and how light pollution or "leaching" can be avoided.

A GREEN DESIGN PROCESS

The following discussion illustrates how to apply these principles and strategies during the various phases of the design process.

PROJECT STARTUP

The first and most important step in practicing green design is making the commitment to do so. Because projects are a kind of dialogue between designers and their clients, it is important that both sides of the partnership embrace a green mission and are willing to support sustainable design principles. In some cases clients have already defined theirs as a green project, with or without specific LEED goals. For example, they may seek to earn LEED points for installing interpretive signage that educates people about the ways that the building saves energy and other resources.

In other cases the graphic designer may have to make the case for a green project and request the extra time or fees necessary to research sustainable materials, standards, processes, and suppliers. While market demand for environmentally friendly products and services has mushroomed, the design industry is still playing catch-up. Some manufacturers and vendors may not be willing or able to answer questions or to provide the exact materials or solutions the designer seeks. It takes extra determination, effort, creative flexibility, and a cooperative client to make a project truly green.

PROGRAMMING SIGN LOCATIONS AND MESSAGES

A good wayfinding designer will specify just the right amount of signage to maximize efficiency with materials and manufacturing. A potential pitfall is the installation of too few signs initially, which may force a costly or cumbersome supplemental retrofit later. As digital wayfinding technologies, such as the global positioning system (GPS), become more advanced and widely available, designers may be able to reduce the quantity of signage by supplementing physical products with electronic media.

The key considerations for signing a built environment are longevity, flexibility, and adaptability. If the use of space is expected to change over time, the design of its signage should enable the elements to be easily replicated and repositioned. Designers can take this a step further in terms of sustainability by designing signs with changeable components to simplify repairs and updates while conserving energy and materials. They should also consider structures that can be easily maintained with simple tools and environmentally friendly cleaners.

In determining sign placement, designers must consider lighting needs and options. A sign can be positioned to take advantage of natural light sources rather than relying on electric lighting for legibility. When illumination is imperative, options such as installing a dimmer or solar generator would be appropriate applications of sustainable design principles.

Paperstone
Paperstone is made from 100 percent postconsumer paper, is formaldehyde free, and has a low-emitting VOC content. This sign sample illustrates direct printing for text and graphics on the raw Paperstone surface. Dimensional letters, with no applied pigments, are adhered using 3M water-based Fastbond.

3form Ecoresin
Ecoresin is made from 40 percent postindustrial waste. 3form offers a reclaim program for pickup and recycling of materials at the end of its life cycle. This test panel consists of three panels of Ecoresin attached with mechanical hardware. This modularity allows for information changes with minimal material waste.

SUSTAINABLE MATERIALS

The most obvious way for a signage designer to make an environmental impact (positive or negative) is through material specification. For optimum sustainability, the materials selected should last for the duration of a sign system's useful life. The longer the expected life span of a design product, the more durable the material needs to be to survive repeated exposure to people and the elements. For example, even though steel panels coated with porcelain enamel may require a good deal of initial energy and expense to produce, they will withstand harsh weather conditions for years. On the other hand, if information content is subject to frequent updating, a highly durable framework combined with a less durable, recyclable panel system offers a more sustainable solution.

Designers should also have some basic knowledge of materials' physical composition and source. Natural materials such as wood, stone, and metals should be reclaimed or sourced locally to reduce the amount of energy expended during manufacturing and transportation. Synthetic materials like acrylic should contain a healthy percentage of recycled content, or be entirely biodegradable. Certain plastics like polypropylene can be easily recycled, while others like polyvinyl chloride (PVC) cannot and take centuries to break down in landfills, releasing harmful chemicals into soil and water in the process. Inks, paints, textiles, and other coatings should contain low (or no) amount of volatile organic compounds (VOCs), which poison the air.

Fortunately, there are many resources available to help designers research and identify the best choices among the thousands of green products on the market today. Reliable sources include the *SEGD Green Paper* and websites of the U.S. Green Building Council, Forest Stewardship Council, Rainforest Alliance, and Green Seal.

Reclaimed Wood

This multilayered sample sign is made of reclaimed, old-growth redwood, formally used in a bridge in Sacramento, California, and overlaid with glass. The glass has sandblasted graphics and is attached with mechanical pins to the base, allowing for modularity and reuse at the end of its life cycle. Redwood is highly durable and flame resistant.

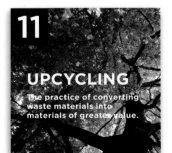

11 UPCYCLING The practice of converting waste materials into materials of greater value.

EverGreen Fabric

Digital printing with solvent or UV inks on fabric that is made from water-based raw materials and contains no extractable heavy metals or carcinogenic or allergenic colorants.

SUSTAINABLE MANUFACTURING AND CONSTRUCTION

An easy way for designers to promote sustainable practices is to build them into the technical requirements of
the Request for Proposal (RFP) or bid document used to
solicit estimates and quotations from fabricators. This
approach makes sustainability a shared responsibility
between designer and sign fabricator.

In general, the key factors in selecting a fabrication
partner who can assist in the goals of sustainability
include location, capabilities, and cooperation: the
closer the fabricator and building products are to the
installation site, the less extraneous material and
energy will be expended in packaging and transportation. The better versed a fabricator is in green
fabrication and mounting methods, the more likely they
are to be used. The easier it is for the designer and the
fabricator to communicate about sustainable practices,
the better they will be at assessing the potential by-
products of manufacturing and how vapors, chemicals,
and scraps might be reduced, reused, or recycled.

DECONSTRUCTION

Designers like to think of their creations as permanent,
but in reality, property changes hands, corporations
merge and fold, and institutions transform themselves
over time or perish. Designers must therefore consider
not only the construction, but also the deconstruction
of their signage designs. Specifying mechanical hardware—simple nuts and bolts, for example—makes for
easy assembly and disassembly and avoids the need
for toxic adhesives. Choosing green materials for all
component parts also ensures that deconstructed signs
can be recycled more effectively.

Designing Green

These two projects reflect
green material choices and
fabrication methods that allow
for eventual deconstruction.
The park sign (top) for Scenic
Hudson, an environmental-
advocacy group, has a frame
and roof structure made from
recycled timbers. The design
of the building-identification
sign (above) for Northern
Arizona University evokes the
local landscape. Its sign panel
(sky) of porcelain enamel was
manufactured using a nontoxic
process that ensures durability
and longevity; the base (earth)
is made of sandstone quarried
locally.

The Civic Sustainability Planner

How can design support sustainability? First of all, planners have to realize that sustainability is a much broader concept than environmentalism because it also encompasses economic growth, which is necessary for human development, and social goals such as health and education.

Designers need to think broadly about the impacts of their projects whether they work on buildings, sign systems, or products. Practicing green design is critical, from using daylighting techniques that maximize natural light in buildings to reducing packaging in consumer goods to enabling the use of recycled materials. It is equally important, though, to consider the ramifications of product life cycles. For instance, the most carbon-efficient building is the one that isn't torn down, so creative reuse represents a more sustainable decision than new construction. Designs that withstand the test of time rather than follow fads will remain in use longer and thus have a lower overall carbon footprint as well as a better economic return.

Designers can also promote this cause by accepting the challenge to make sustainable projects more attractive. Good design encourages neighborhoods to accept local facilities such as power plants. Distributing power generation among many smaller plants is more efficient than relying on large plants with long transmission lines, so this represents a contribution to the environment. Similarly, it is critical to make green products appealing for reasons beyond their sustainability; even with gasoline at record prices, a poorly designed hybrid car will not sell. The user-friendly graphic design of New York's sustainability plan, PlaNYC, is another example. In this case, a lively and readable presentation engages broader audiences and stimulates greater excitement about the city's ideas than a less attractive design.

Finally, designers may have to challenge their clients to think sustainably. Specifying glass walls and bright lobby lighting may be the norm for office construction today, but it is not inherently the most efficient approach. Designers should try to educate their clients about considering more environmentally responsible choices.

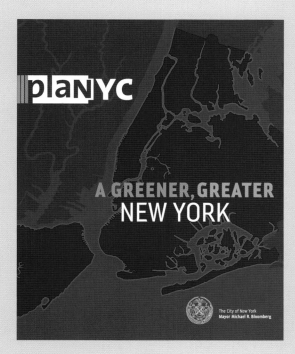

The good news is that well-designed solutions pay off. This is apparent because the marketplace is beginning to value sustainable design as the public becomes more environmentally aware about their buying decisions. The other benefit is that sustainable design is economically as well as environmentally sound. As the price of construction materials, transportation, and energy all increase over the long-term, designs that consume fewer resources will not only help the environment but also save the client money. It may take a little education, but designers who make the effort to think sustainably and inform their clients should find a receptive audience.

Rohit Aggarwala is the Director of Long-term Planning and Sustainability for the City of New York in the Mayor's Office of Operations.

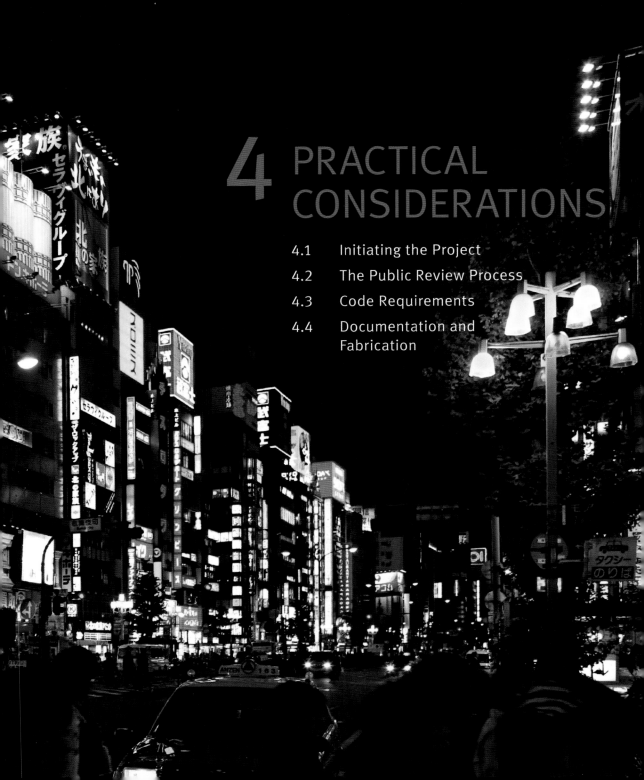

4 PRACTICAL CONSIDERATIONS

4.1
INITIATING THE PROJECT

So that's all for a beginning.
On to the meat of the matter!
JULIA CHILD, *JULIA CHILD AND COMPANY*

Successful wayfinding design is like dialogue, a form of conversation between client and designer. Because many signage projects last several years, a short-term dialogue can evolve into a long-term relationship. As discussed in chapter 1.3, the client is usually a collection of people and interests, while the designer is a team of professionals from different disciplines. The beginning of the project is the time to define parameters, get to know everyone, and set everything in motion.

LEARN ABOUT
How the client plans a project and selects a wayfinding designer

For clients the project begins when they decide to undertake it, which activates a series of related tasks: defining the scope, including goals and time frame, assembling the committee to manage the design effort, seeking funding for design and construction, and selecting a designer. The more clearly these aspects are defined, the easier it will be for the designers to begin their work. The Request for Proposal (known as an RFP in the trade, see page 132) is the client's opportunity to define the project so that designers can respond with a design-services proposal and bid for the work.

In the proposal, a designer has to exhibit an understanding of the project and how it can be undertaken. A proposal reiterates the scope, defines an approach, outlines the team and roles, describes the process, and sets a price for the work. After reviewing submissions, the client often follows up by interviewing a short list of design teams, then the project committee reviews the presentations and makes a selection. Client and designer then negotiate the contract so that the actual work can begin.

THE CLIENT DEFINES THE PROJECT

In some cases the final product is simple—just one sign for an individual storefront or a sign program for a small building—and does not require substantial explanation from the client or extensive preliminary analysis on the designer's part to prepare a proposal. More involved assignments, such as an urban transit system or a wayfinding program for a mixed-use retail entertainment center, require greater attention or input from both client and designer.

For the client to define the scope of any project, he or she must address certain questions: What kinds of signs are needed and where might they be installed? What are the visitor or customer requirements? What are the owner or management requirements? To answer the questions, the client should consult peers, talk with planners and architects already working on the project, and survey related environments. Extensive investigation enables the client to understand all aspects of the project and its component parts in order to draft a concise definition of scope. This definition states detailed guidelines for the designer to follow in preparing a design-services proposal and provides a benchmark against which the completed project can eventually be measured.

SEEKING FUNDING AND SUPPORT

In addition to providing the basis for the RFP, the project definition helps build management support for the undertaking. For existing spaces the definition folds in a discussion of wayfinding problems that already exist. For new building projects, it reminds the project design and construction team that signage is necessary and must be included in the overall budget.

As support for the project grows, financial planning or fundraising should begin. For major building projects, the budget for signage must be carved out of the capital set aside for the entire project. A signage budget has two major components: design costs and fabrication or construction costs. Sometimes the project begins with only enough money for design fees and expenses; once design is underway the client can raise construction money from public or private sources. The design process helps the client build a more articulate argument for signage. It also generates illustrations and presentation materials that support the financing or fundraising appeals.

ASSEMBLING THE PROJECT COMMITTEES

Having the right client committee structure to run a project is critical. In many cases, a series of committees is necessary to direct a project smoothly and get the necessary approvals. Though each organization has its own culture and requirements, in general there are three groups: the core signage or wayfinding committee, to manage the project; the stakeholders group, to provide input; and the management team, to give the necessary approvals and provide feedback. Each committee will vary somewhat by project. These are general functions required for most large-scale wayfinding projects:

The wayfinding committee is a group that often averages five to ten people who function collectively as the client. It is led by the project manager—the point person or day-to-day project coordinator—and has representatives of the key constituencies (see page 130) with an interest in the signage project. This group reviews the work in progress and provides regular feedback to the design team. The wayfinding committee can provide consistent feedback and a degree of continuity during the life of the project.

The stakeholders group is a more loosely defined cluster of people that provide additional input and feedback during the design process. They might be members of the client organization with useful opinions and information, or they might represent outside organizations that will benefit from or participate in the signage program in some way. Discussions with the stakeholders group ensure that the wayfinding system will meet the needs of a larger community. This group can be assembled early on to provide facts and details, or later to provide alternate opinions during work-in-progress design reviews.

The management team is the individual or group of people, such as the officers of a university or the CEO of a corporation, who have the larger corporate or institutional perspective and provide final approvals. The project manager's experience and savvy determines the best time to engage the management team, whether at the beginning or near the end after decisions have been made and the design is resolved. A simple nod from the management team moves the project forward and confirms that the client organization as a whole has embraced the plan.

4.1

University Campus Wayfinding Project Committees

The following is the committee structure for a typical university- or college-campus wayfinding design project.

WAYFINDING COMMITTEE
Directly overseeing and representing several different disciplines, this committee helps ensure that the review of the designer's work in progress is comprehensive and reflects diverse perspectives.
- Project Manager
- University Architect
- Director of Public Affairs
- Director of Design and Communications
- Associate Facilities Manager
- Professor of History of Art

STAKEHOLDERS GROUP
This group is called upon to provide input, statistics, and background information. Constituencies not included in the wayfinding committee are represented here so that the signage systems will take into account the broad range of issues that the institution faces.
- Director of Student Activities
- Associate Provost for Academic Affairs
- Assistant Director of Athletics
- Manager of Support Services
- Director of Campus Security
- Dean of Admissions
- Director of Marketing
- Manager of Buildings and Grounds
- Head of the Student Senate

MANAGEMENT TEAM
These are the leaders of the university whose final approval ensures that the system has the support of the institutional leadership throughout the implementation process.
- University President
- Vice President of Finance and Administration
- University Secretary
- Director of Development
- Dean of Architecture
- Chair of the Board of Trustees Building and Grounds Committee

THE SELECTION PROCESS
Sometimes selecting an environmental graphic design scheme is quite simple. The client just calls a colleague and asks him or her to design a particular project, agrees to a fee, and begins. In most cases, however, standard business practices or official regulations require the client to seek competing bids or proposals. The selection process is often handled in one of two ways. In one model, a Request for Qualifications (RFQ) is issued. In this case, designers are asked to provide information about their firm, key personnel, and relevant project experience. The client committee reviews the submissions and selects a handful of qualified competitors, who are then asked to prepare a process and fee proposal in response to an RFP or to an in-person interview, sometimes both. Based on the submissions, the fees, the design-team interview, and the testimony or references, the client selects a firm.

A more streamlined approach is to send out a comprehensive RFP that asks designers to lay out firm and team qualifications, a detailed discussion of the team's approach to the project, and the proposed work process and cost estimates. A shortlist of finalists is then selected based on these submissions. As above, the finalists may be interviewed, and references checked before a decision is made.

The final stage of the selection process is contract negotiations. The client and the selected designer review the details of scope, process, and fees, as well as related issues such as insurance, payment terms, and intellectual property issues. When an agreement is reached, the contract is signed and the project begins.

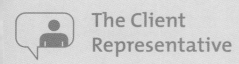

The Client Representative

When the Charlotte Department of Transportation in North Carolina initiated a search for a wayfinding consultant to improve navigation in the city's center, we quickly narrowed down our selection to a few firms with the best design qualifications and most extensive experience. The search proceeded smoothly because Charlotte's government is well run, and there is a wonderful city manager. Every major project is guided by a steering committee with representatives from the departments that have a stake in its outcome. The city also has an established communications process that makes it easy for outside consultants to get feedback about their work. So by marshalling in-house resources and encouraging everyone to participate early on, there's better "buy-in." This applies to any decision, whether hiring a consultant or seeking stakeholders' approval for a design.

The steering committee for Charlotte's wayfinding project developed an RFQ in close collaboration with the procurement department and advertised it as widely as possible to the EGD community. We selected our wayfinding consultant solely based on qualifications. What convinced us? The quality of the firm's response to the RFQ, our interview with key players, and their assurances about which staff members would be assigned to the project.

While any materials submitted in response to a government RFQ must conform exactly to stated requirements, this constraint should not prevent designers from designing a handsome package for the submission. Conscientious and creative bidders can really stand out from the competition by delivering a beautifully designed document that looks great on an executive's desk.

We were very fortunate to receive state and federal funding for this wayfinding project from programs dedicated to congestion management. Other municipalities might be interested to know that we applied for and received over five million dollars by demonstrating that improved navigation

will have a major impact on air quality by reducing car trips. A related goal has been to make Charlotte's ample parking easy to find. In fact, one of our key operating principles is that no matter how you get around Uptown—Charlotte's name for its downtown—at least part of your trip will be on foot.

Howard Landers, AICP, is a consultant to the Department of Transportation for Charlotte, North Carolina. He managed the planning study to improve the city's downtown and is currently deputy project manager for wayfinding.

THE CLIENT'S REQUEST FOR PROPOSAL

Both public and private clients develop RFPs to outline the specifics of a wayfinding-design assignment. The level of detail in an RFP can vary tremendously. Some RFPs are simple, just a few pages describing project intent and bid request. These allow the greatest creative flexibility, but as designers try to interpret the client's priorities, they may have many questions about schedule, budget, and scope. An RFP may run up to eighty pages or more, much of it covering contractual issues that need to be read and understood.

The best RFPs are clear, succinct, and well organized and provide basic information about the client and why the project is being commissioned. They describe the physical boundaries of the property, often including maps or plans, and state key challenges for wayfinding and signage. They name any other consultants or decision-makers involved and key stakeholder groups that will need to be engaged. They outline the anticipated phases of the project and provide specific time frames or deadlines. Some clients may state the project budget or sources of funding; others prefer to keep this information confidential until contract award. The RFP also dictates the form and structure of the proposal document as well as any application instructions and deadlines.

Most organizations also allow for a question period after the RFP is issued, compiling questions from respondents, then issuing a single "answer" document to everyone several days in advance of the proposal due date. Others prefer to answer respondents' questions individually.

THE DESIGNER'S RESPONSE TO THE RFP

In the rare case that a project is offered exclusively to one designer, the designer must be ready and able to start immediately and provide a reasonable fee proposal for the effort. The selection process is usually a competition, however, so the design firm has to invest time and resources just to win the project—a hardship for small firms.

Submitting a thoughtful and complete response shows respect for the client's needs and process and facilitates fair evaluation. As creative professionals,

designers may be tempted to break the mold and submit proposals in an unusual form or manner to catch attention. This approach might be effective if the client is able to assess wildly divergent proposals. In most situations, though, it is prudent to follow RFP requirements to the letter. Government agencies are particularly unforgiving and will discard a bid outright if it arrives even a minute overdue, omits any required information, or violates format restrictions in any way.

RFP Table of Contents

This sample table of contents for a client's RFP is comprehensive but not all-inclusive. All of the following points may or may not be included since the level of detail varies from project to project, client to client.

BACKGROUND
Client/project team
Existing conditions and site description
Project goals/objectives

SCOPE OF WORK
Project geography and boundaries
Anticipated elements of the project
Tasks to be handled by consultant
Project phasing and schedule, or target completion date
Budget information (if available)
Anticipated formula for fee calculation: hourly fee,
    lump sum, percent of construction budget, etc.

SUBMISSION REQUIREMENTS
Required content and format
Recipient address and contact information
Deadline instructions

CONTRACTUAL REQUIREMENTS
Staffing quotas
Technical specifications
Required meetings and reviews
Deliverables
Affirmative-action targets (if applicable)

APPENDICES
Relevant documents such as renderings, floor plans
Design/construction schedule
Sample contract

The Marketing Director

What's special about marketing wayfinding-design services? Environmental graphic design is such a niche business that after the first cut in a pitch or proposal process, you usually vie against peers. These are all highly qualified firms with similar experience and capabilities, so it is very competitive. What also distinguishes wayfinding from other graphic design services? The prospective client often requires that the proposed work process, particularly for building projects, follow a standard structure based on phases common to architecture. This helps clients compare "apples to apples" when evaluating bids.

Since the competition is fierce and the work process is largely predetermined, strategy becomes the key to success. You win or lose based on how you approach the assignment, the expertise of your team, and your fee structure. You need to show the prospective client how seriously you've thought about their project, introduce the people who would work on it, and clearly explain what you propose to deliver for the budget.

To develop a winning approach, you must not only address the client's challenge but understand their own grasp of it. Have they clearly defined the problem, or do you need to add a robust analysis phase to do that with them? If a client wants schematic design to start right after the first briefing, you may need to argue persuasively for an additional research-and-analysis budget in order to gain a deeper understanding of the issues that will inform a creative strategy.

Having the right personnel can win a contract, so the marketing group has to put together an appropriate mix of talent from within the firm, and perhaps outside it. Some-times, though, you have to make a quick judgment call about choosing the right team members just to get a proposal out the door. In other cases, you may have taken great care to put together a winning team, but by the time the job actually starts, a key person is no longer available to work on it. That is obviously not ideal for the client relationship, but it happens, and when it does, it is better that it happens before a job starts than after work has begun. No one likes to change horses midstream.

To meet the qualifications of an RFP, you may need to partner with another person or company that offers a complementary service, such as structural engineering, or provides a local presence. You might also tap into the expertise of specialists such as urban planners, map and type designers, illustrators, traffic engineers, communications consultants, or specification writers. That's when a network of contacts built up over the course of a career becomes invaluable. The larger and more sophisticated the firm, though, the more important it becomes to invest in a database for that information. I can't overemphasize the importance of good information asset management. You have to keep databases and archives up-to-date with current photography, project descriptions, past proposals, staff biographies, and contacts. This material is the lifeblood of marketing, and it needs to keep flowing.

Sarah Haun, director of marketing and communications for Two Twelve Associates, has over twenty years' experience working in the design industry as a business communications and marketing specialist.

Designers generally provide three kinds of information in proposals for wayfinding projects: technical, cost-related, and firm qualifications.

The technical proposal affirms the designer's interest in the project, interprets the assignment, and outlines an approach or philosophy for addressing it.

This upfront sell opportunity allows a design firm to convince the client that their knowledge and perspective is deeper than the other bidders'. The technical proposal also confirms the specific scope of work to be included in and excluded from the designer's proposed fee-and-expenses budget, and addresses it through the project phases. The work plan describes associated tasks and deliverables for each phase and includes a schedule or time frames for completion.

Drafting the pricing proposal with budgets for fees and expenses requires mathematical skill and good judgment—a complex subject that could easily fill another book. In a typical case, the proposal writer first determines who will do the work, then estimates how many hours each person will spend on their task. The rough fee is then calculated by multiplying those hours by the person's hourly rate. (Rates typically cover the person's salary and benefits costs, plus a portion of the firm's overhead as calculated by the firm's accountant.) The number may be presented to the client as is or rounded up or down as appropriate to meet market demands. On top of the fees, a line item may be added to cover out-of-pocket expenses such as local travel costs, couriers, and supplies. The estimator must take RFP requirements into account and have an informed opinion about what the market will bear: What is the real value of the work to the client? Do they have deep pockets or will they have to raise funds? Will time sheets and receipts have to be submitted or can the project be billed as a lump sum? Clients often accept or reject proposals on the basis of price alone, so it is important to make sure that fees are competitive, clearly explained, and well justified. The designer may include general terms of agreement or a standard contract if requested, or these may be brought forward during the open project-award negotiation process.

The firm qualifications section (quals) describes the proposed project team and structure, naming key individuals and their relevant experience. It explains how different team members will work together and interact with the client. It provides background information about the firm and any subconsultants or partners who may be involved. The qualifications also typically includes information about the team's relevant work experience, such as a client list, descriptions and visual documentation of past projects, and contact information for client references. In some cases prospective clients will request copies of financial documents such as an overhead or profit-and-loss

statement, balance sheet, certificate of insurance, or other third-party evidence of the business's solvency and professional track record.

Within the given parameters, the proposal also needs to convey the firm's design aesthetic and intellectual approach. The document should be organized and include thoughtfully considered wayfinding devices, such as a table of contents, section dividers, and appendices for larger documents, to help the client navigate the information. Any organizational charts, project sheets, and other visual materials must be coordinated and present a coherent picture of the respondent's capabilities. The text should be clear business-writing style, carefully proofread—and the math double-checked—prior to final printing.

Proposal Table Of Contents

The table of contents for a design proposal must follow what the RFP dictates as exactly as possible. The following items are usually included:

TECHNICAL PROPOSAL
Project background
Goals/objectives
Design approach
Team/organizational chart
Scope of work list
Work plan and schedule
Budget, fees, and expenses
Contractual terms

QUALIFICATIONS
Design-firm description
Biographies of key personnel
Relevant project experience
Client references

4.2
THE PUBLIC REVIEW PROCESS

Unless each individual develops a sense of responsibility,
the whole community cannot move. So therefore it is very
essential that we should not feel that individual effort
is meaningless.
DALAI LAMA XIV, *THE DALAI LAMA'S LITTLE BOOK OF WISDOM*

Large, multifaceted projects send the designer down a more circuitous path than smaller ones. They usually require the designer to analyze layers of information and formulate strategies that typically affect multiple stakeholders. Because these strategies can also impact the public realm, designers must be adept at managing the communications, making presentations, and building the consensus necessary to secure a project go-ahead. While the designer must take the lead throughout the creative process, he or she should also engage others in order to gain support and approval for ideas as they are being developed. These interactions encompass stakeholder interviews, client presentations, community reviews, management buy-in, staff support, public-agency reviews, and civic commission approvals.

LEARN ABOUT
The communications required to
complete a wayfinding project

During the early research and programming phases of a project, it is essential that the designer meet all stakeholders and hear concerns about what might affect wayfinding design for their particular site. For civic wayfinding, those stakeholders might include representatives of neighborhoods, community organizations, or key destinations that will benefit. Stakeholders in hospitals come from different departments such as security, public affairs, visitor services, patient care, public affairs, development, facilities, and maintenance. In both instances, the design team conducts interviews to gather inside opinions about current wayfinding problems as well as to understand the visitor's experience. Ongoing dialogue with stakeholders helps to test ideas and ensure that strategies under consideration are viable.

Throughout the creative process—when the designer conducts research and analysis, develops strategies, and generates visual ideas—presentations for the client are necessary and significant milestones, and periodic reviews help a designer gain support on an incremental basis. Often, the client who attends presentations is actually a group of people representing different constituencies. For example, in a downtown wayfinding project, the design team makes interim presentations to the community; these large and diverse meetings give representatives of different organizations the chance to see how the design is developing and provide input. These meetings often function along the lines of an informal focus group where personal opinions are shared. As this type of open forum can be overwhelming to a designer who is too heavily invested in a single great idea that he or she wants to sell, it is best to keep the dialogue focused on strategy and purpose.

Needless to say, presentation quality is important. With experience the designer will develop an increasingly sophisticated vocabulary of presentation techniques. Though hand-drawn sketches are appropriate for idea generation, clients expect to see computer-generated illustrations when reviewing schematic designs. At first these can be simple elevations and views of sign elements. As the ideas become more complex and the details are developed, three-dimensional renderings are useful to demonstrate how signs will integrate with the architectural setting and give clients a more accurate picture of the designer's intention.

Many projects need management buy-in. This is usually an intimate process that allows the designer and client project manager to meet privately with a VIP, such as the mayor, a CEO, or organizational leader, to present the project and win approval for the final program. A positive nod from the top usually smoothes the way for the project and ensures organizational support for the proposed design direction.

With a completed design and support from management in hand, the next step is to build staff consensus. Earning staff endorsement is particularly useful for wayfinding systems that introduce innovative ways of communicating, such as new nomenclature for different areas within the hospital or a new strategy and system for public wayfinding. Dialogue with key team leaders in the organization is necessary if the staff is to understand and embrace the new design approach. Publishing articles and announcements in employee newsletters is an effective way to build momentum for a wayfinding program's launch, especially if it is going to introduce a new visual identity or institutional branding.

For most large urban environmental graphic design projects, public agency reviews will be necessary. These reviews usually involve the local department of transportation responsible for signing and infrastructure on city streets. Typically, they are information sessions that provide a forum to share the work in progress with city engineers, and their main purpose is to confirm compliance with city codes and regulations and gain consensus for the design. In some cases it may be necessary to apply for special permits.

Certain jurisdictions, particularly those in large cities, require approvals by special public commissions. These often involve a formal hearing and/or a presentation before commissioners; after a discussion period, they vote on the proposal. These encounters can be frustrating, especially when the designer—charged with presenting a compelling argument for the programmatic strategy and actual designs—must convince a diverse and sometimes skeptical group of commissioners. In

New York City, for example, there are two such groups: the Landmarks Preservation Commission, which is responsible for identifying and designating the city's landmark buildings and districts and for reviewing projects that will affect or alter them, and the Art Commission, which reviews works of art, architecture, and landscape architecture proposed for city-owned property.

Sometimes all these reviews and approvals seem a little overwhelming—a never-ending maze of meetings and false starts. But handled patiently and persistently with dedication to good design principles, this process guarantees a wayfinding system's enthusiastic and universal adoption and ensures that all the goals of the client organization are addressed.

4.3
CODE
REQUIREMENTS

The care of human life and happiness, and not their destruction, is the first and only legitimate object of good government.

THOMAS JEFFERSON, 1809 *SPEECH*

Apart from the aesthetic, functional, and business considerations necessary for good wayfinding design, the designer also needs to be aware of certain legal requirements. Because legislation is subject to change, this chapter identifies three areas of research that designers must undertake to ensure that a wayfinding system meets necessary legal and current standards.

LEARN ABOUT
How legal issues impact wayfinding design

AMERICANS WITH DISABILITIES ACT

The ADA legislation, passed for the first time in 1990, mandates specific graphic and architectural standards for new and renovated facilities across the country. At its inception it served as a wake-up call, forcing designers to become more proactive about solving problems faced by people with disabilities. Until then, people with visual, auditory, and other physical challenges faced barriers to access or comfortable navigation in facilities.

The Society for Environmental Graphic Design (SEGD) has been instrumental in educating designers about the ADA's impact on wayfinding, keeping them abreast of new legislation and encouraging them to comply with the most creative solutions possible. The organization regularly publishes the *Americans with Disabilities Act White Paper*, to explain current legislation and how designers can ensure that their sign system designs comply with federal guidelines. The guidelines address sign location, overhead clearance, sizing and styling of letters for key sign types, required figure-field contrast, tactile and Braille lettering, mapping, special accessibility symbols, and other variables. Together, these guidelines serve as a primer about key design considerations that affect people's access to specific types of spaces and their sensory experience of them.

LOCAL SIGN CODES

Wayfinding designers working in different regions also have to be aware of local codes. To regulate the size and quantity of outdoor signage, some municipalities have developed exterior signage guidelines. These might describe where signs can be located—how high off the ground or how close to roadways and property lines they can be placed, for example. They might also define the square footage allowed for signs in a particular location and whether signs can be illuminated. It is the designer's responsibility to research local sign codes so that a particular project will meet legal requirements. For new construction projects, the architects are often a good resource for advice and information as they are already familiar with local code issues. Designers also hire code consultants to interpret regulations or to assist in applying for a variance.

FIRE- AND LIFE-SAFETY REGULATIONS

The other major area of code compliance is that of fire and life safety. There are specific requirements for the signing and egress mapping of stairwells and elevators. Designers must understand the appropriate local, state, and federal legal requirements in order to create compliant solutions; project architects and team code specialists can be useful sources of information. The National Fire Protection Association has great resources on fire codes and signing requirements (available at www.nfpa.org).

4.4
DOCUMENTATION AND FABRICATION

An artist is not simply a person with ideas.
He is a person who has the skill to make
his ideas manifest.
ERIC GILL, *ART AND A CHANGING CIVILIZATION*

This chapter reviews three activities that occur near the end of the design and implementation phases of a wayfinding system: creating a sign documentation package, holding a bidding process to select a sign fabrication company, and supervising fabrication and installation.

LEARN ABOUT
Creating a bidding package for fabricators

THE SIGN-DOCUMENTATION PACKAGE

Once all the elements of a wayfinding strategy are established—every sign's location and message, the overriding design direction, graphic and three-dimensional styling, custom structures, and media design—it is time to create electronic files for a set of technical documents known as design-intent drawings. The purpose of this type of documentation is to record and explain all design decisions so that prospective sign fabricators can prepare estimates for fabrication and installation. These documents provide a comprehensive overview of the entire wayfinding system, spelling out what the fabricator needs to know in order to build and install all components. Most of the materials in the sign-documentation package are technical drawings of the front, top, and side views

of signs. The drawings also show how the nonvisible interior sign components are constructed. Wayfinding designers must learn how to create these drawings to the correct scale so that they can be properly interpreted by sign fabricators.

Design-intent drawings spell out how the signs will look and how they will function, without determining each and every connection or detail. This set of drawings allows experienced sign fabricators some leeway in the system's execution and permits them to recommend the best approach. By specifically classifying these drawings as design-intent documents, the designer entrusts the fabricator with quality control. That company then bears responsibility for the system's overall integrity by assuming authorship of all final detailing and engineering, and manufacturing the actual product. Sign-documentation packages usually include these standard contents:

Sign-type List
The sign-type list is exactly what it sounds like: a simple listing of all categories of signs. The list is usually organized by exterior or interior signage and categorized by type, such as identification, direction, orientation, regulation, etc. Each sign type is assigned a letter or number code, so that all details for a particular sign can be referenced (see chapter 2.4).

Graphic Standards
The designer spells out the program's typographic standards by showing the specific weights, slope, and sizes of the fonts selected for signage. Likewise, any symbols or special graphics, need to be documented. Custom graphic elements must be supplied as electronic files to the fabrication company. It is useful to provide reference where special project fonts may be purchased.

Sign-location Plans
By this stage, the designer will have completed the sign-programming phase (see chapter 2.4). The work is then checked once more before submission for client approval. Final sign location plans covering the full scope of the project site should be included in the document package.

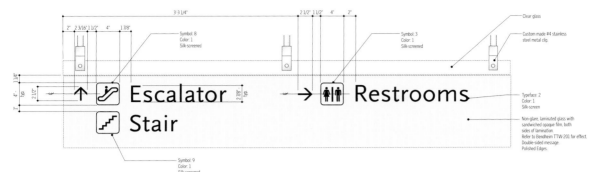

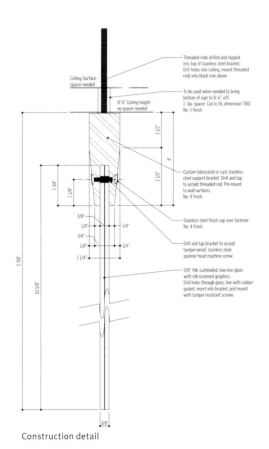

Sign-panel layout

Construction detail

Sign-message Schedule

As the designer completes sign location plans, he or she refines the sign-message schedule by replacing interim or draft messages with final versions. Once the team checks and approves the sign-message schedule, it can be added to the documentation (see chapter 2.4).

Sign-panel Layouts

These drawings record all details for every sign-panel layout. The signage typography and the specific locations of each message are spelled out. Graphics are dimensioned and the use of different colors notated. A layout drawing must be supplied for each of the different kinds of panels in the overall system.

Sign-layout Artwork

In certain instances the designer creates an electronic file for every sign layout. This level of specificity for artwork is only possible for smaller wayfinding programs with a limited number of signs. It may also be necessary for unique signs with a special function or in a system where signs are so different from each other that it is not possible to provide templates of typical layouts.

Construction Details

The construction drawings describe the physical structure of the signs and explain how to build, construct, finish, and attach them. The number and complexity of these detail drawings will depend on the scale of the project and the variety of details from sign type to sign type. Whenever possible, the designer should consider standardizing the details throughout the system. This will simplify the fabrication process and can help contain costs.

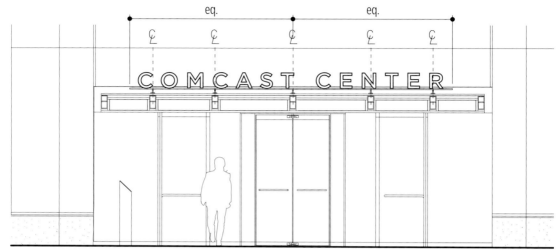

Sign-installation elevation

Sign-installation Elevations

Another set of drawings defines how the signs will be located in the space, and at what height they will be mounted. Whenever possible, standard mounting protocols should be determined and documented in the sign package. Otherwise, each unique condition will also need to be recorded.

Sign Specifications

This document describes the anticipated standards of construction, quality of materials, and installation standards expected of the sign fabricator. The specifications also list submittals to be delivered by the fabricator, such as shop drawings (see page 142), color or material samples, and actual sign prototypes. Typically, the cost of sign prototypes is built into the fabrication estimate. These prototypes allow each sign type to be tested in actual materials prior to fabrication.

Instructions to Bidders

The sign document package is, in fact, an exhaustively illustrated guideline for a bid process that involves a select group of fabricators. It is helpful to advise the prospective bidders about the format expected for their submission—for instance, how the cost figures must be structured. All bidders receive a specific form to fill out with their price quotation; a uniform presentation vastly simplifies vendor cost comparison.

The Sign Fabricator

When should a designer consult a fabricator? The earlier, the better, for all involved. Even before the design contract is awarded, a reliable fabricator can suggest new materials or technologies that might give the designer a competitive advantage. Working closely together early on can also ensure that designs stay within budget or, if not, provide time to cost-engineer alternatives.

I'm always amazed by the number of designers (or their clients) who won't share budget information, which forces sign-specification development to occur in a vacuum and generates unnecessary work. The designer may create the "ultimate sign system" only to find the materials are outrageously expensive, or the fabrication method is too labor intensive, or both. Hours of design time and often very expensive custom samples then get sacrificed when the client goes into sticker shock. When an experienced fabricator understands the budget, he can suggest appropriate materials and techniques ahead of time, and even make engineering recommendations.

We highly recommend establishing a collaborative design-build venture with a well-established fabricator known for quality work and good project management. If the fabricator is intimately familiar with the end product, specifications and drawings can also be streamlined. Furthermore, the client is then spared the substantial cost of preparing detailed bid documents and managing a competitive bid process.

If the client insists on a bid process, the designer should advise against automatically selecting the lowest bidder, often a contractor who is blind to quality differences. Because signs are typically the last things to be installed in a new building prior to opening, the client may accept substandard ones in a rush just to secure a Certificate of Occupancy (C of O). Any poor work or sloppy installation by the fabricator inevitably reflects badly on the designer;

by recommending only qualified fabricators, the designer can convince a client to spend a little more for a higher quality product. Sign fabrication is more of an art than a science, so there is tremendous variation between vendors. Consequently, the designer should insist on obtaining key sign type samples to check their quality of workmanship—the investment is usually worthwhile.

Another point of comparison between fabricators is their ability to deliver a green product. Visual Graphic Systems excels at sourcing sustainable materials and developing greener manufacturing techniques. We've invested in Durst Rho equipment that digitally prints directly onto rigid materials using UV-cured inks, thereby eliminating wasted ink and, more importantly, solvents. Printing directly onto the surface of sustainable substrates, such as Plyboo, eliminates the need for costly, less environmentally friendly adhesives or lamination plastics. We've also switched from spray painting metal surfaces to powder coating them, a more environmentally friendly process.

Committing to green practices requires the entire company's cooperation, so we educate our staff about ways to be more environmentally responsible. For instance, the advantage of a green material may be offset if the fuel used for its transportation is excessive. A sign constructed of aluminum, wood, and plastic is only recyclable if it can be easily disassembled. A design should also take a sign's anticipated life cycle into account: it may be preferable in the long run to use a less sustainable but more durable material, such as stainless steel, to extend an exterior sign's longevity.

Donall Healy is chairman and CEO of Visual Graphic Systems (VGS) in New York City. His career in architectural signing began in 1977 when, as president of Letraset USA, he cofounded ASI Sign Systems, a national network of architectural sign fabricators. Healy holds over a half dozen patents in the sign and display field.

BUDGETING FOR FABRICATION AND INSTALLATION

Clients need to review estimates for fabrication at several points during the design process. This allows the team to set a budget if none exists, or to confirm that predetermined budget goals are being met. Early on, budget estimates are rough, based on projections of sign counts and ballpark fabrication estimates determined even before specific signs are designed. Once the design process is underway, the designer begins a dialogue with potential fabricators to develop more specific interim price estimates in advance of the formal bid process. Installation costs are calculated as 15 to 20 percent of the fabrication budget at this stage.

THE BID PROCESS

When the time comes to select a fabricator, the design-intent documents serve as the primary tool for soliciting bids. Often, because they do not want to pay designers to lead the effort, clients manage the formal solicitation and review of bids from sign fabricators. The designer, then, plays an advisory role by providing a list of recommended bidders, answering questions that might arise, and helping to review the bids received. The designer ensures that the bids demonstrate an understanding of the project's parameters. Once the client and designer identify the best response from the bidding pool—one that combines strong qualifications, the most thorough response, and the best price— the project is awarded.

FABRICATION SUPERVISION

After becoming completely familiar with the documents in order to develop a plan for execution, the selected company embarks on two distinct phases of work: fabrication and installation. It is important that the fabricator make its own measurements and calculations, before starting to manufacture as they bear ultimate responsibility and liability for manufacturing the wayfinding system correctly. To this end, the fabricator prepares a set of shop drawings for the designer and client that show exactly how the actual signs will be fabricated.

Inspecting large-scale letter fabrication

Exterior letterforms prior to installation

Fabricating map-dispenser box

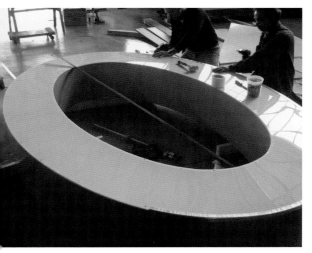
Fabricating large exterior letterforms

Internally illuminated sign face

INSTALLATION SUPERVISION

Once every element of a system is built, the fabricator must install them. The designer usually assists at this stage by specifying precise sign locations. The installer must follow the designer's instructions to the letter, placing the correct sign or structure exactly where specified. The designer visits the site at the beginning of the process to confirm that everything is going according to plan. For a large-scale installation, periodic project site inspections are appropriate. Upon completion the designer conducts a final review of the installation and creates a punch list, a detailed tally of all the problems such as damaged signs in need of repair, or reinstallation and other miscellaneous corrections the sign company needs to make to fulfill their contractual obligations.

Entry beacon being delivered to the building site

At this stage the fabricator also provides color and material samples to ensure that the design specifications have been followed precisely. This process often takes a few passes, and the designer may need to visit the shop several times in order to review fabrication samples, check the quality of the workmanship, and determine that the fabricator has followed the documents precisely. It is essential that the designer make a final review of key prototypes before everything is built to verify that the actual signs match the approved designs and to correct flaws in the design or the fabrication process. With the sign-off in hand, the fabricator begins to manufacture the full system.

AFTER THE WAYFINDING SYSTEM IS COMPLETED

In many cases the wayfinding designer's work is done once a sign system is built and installed and the punch list of problems has been addressed. At this stage the client and facility management team take on the responsibility of maintaining the system and updating it as necessary.

In some cases the designer will complete just a prototypical installation for a key portion of the facility. For instance, in some new large-scale commercial developments where wayfinding will eventually be required throughout, signs may be installed only where construction is already complete. The client then contracts for additional sign installations as necessary for later construction phases. In the case of a medical complex, the first round of wayfinding implementation might apply only to a section of a hospital or just one building. For urban wayfinding, signs might be installed experimentally in one district. Once tested to everyone's satisfaction, an entire system can then be rolled out in phases as resources become available.

For large projects that require ongoing implemen-tation over several years, a signage manual is essential. This manual describes the entire wayfinding system, including an overview of key individual elements; a description of their function and how they are used; exact standards for locating signs and crafting sign messages; and drawings similar to those in the sign-documentation package. This invaluable reference enables clients to supervise further application of the system once the preliminary installation phase is complete. Likewise, the manual guides system main-tenance, ensuring that new signs or replacements for damaged ones conform to system standards.

The traditional sign manual is a letter-sized document, printed and bound for easy handling and storage by facility management. Driven by the expan-sion of the web and people's preference for online information, organizations are beginning to post sign manuals in PDF form on the internet so that the information is easily accessible. It is also possible to turn a web-based manual into an interactive tool that allows a sign manager to track inventories and verify the look and the content of specific signs before they are ordered, somewhat analogous to web shopping sites where items can be customized in patterns and colors prior to ordering. Online signage manuals can also allow individual users to access the system, look for a specific sign type, enter the required copy, and then order what they need. Databases can also be programmed to assign new sign type codes and track additions to the system.

Wayfinding systems serve living environments where functions for areas change, spaces are renovated, and new facilities are constructed. Designers must create systems that are flexible and adapt to the evolution of a place. Once their work is complete, they should leave behind a comprehensive, and comprehensible, record of their work to ensure that the wayfinding system is sustainable over the long haul.

ACKNOWLEDGMENTS

Creating *The Wayfinding Handbook: Information Design for Public Places* was truly a collaborative effort in every way. I am most grateful to Juanita Dugdale, my editorial consultant and former business partner, who helped guide this book to completion. She vetted my ideas, added more than a few of her own, and read and edited everything I wrote. I particularly appreciate her help in crafting the introductory chapter and the "Other Voices" sidebar commentaries by my colleagues and friends. This book would not have been possible without her.

Laura Varacchi, one of the very capable creative leaders at Two Twelve Associates, working with Vijay Mathews and Julie Park, brought the book to life with her elegant and informative design. The design team contributed not only the design and production of the book but also found and/or shaped many of the images. Sarah Haun, another colleague at Two Twelve Associates, was an able supporter and mentor to this process and the product. She helped me articulate the concept for the book and made significant contributions to the process. Likewise, thanks to Katie Baker for her help in assembling Two Twelve Associates' materials for the book. Anthony Ferrara and his great team of wayfinding designers, including Dominic Borgia, Karuna Hernandez, Alexandria Lee, Chris Dina, Darlene Levy, Maura Mathews, Corey Mintz, and Andy Ng, helped me turn our collective experience into the content for a textbook. Special thanks to Dominic for his help with materials and processes. My able assistant, Grace Moreno-Vasquez, did an amazing job of gathering the images for the book and securing permissions. Jess Mackta, our project manager, valiantly worked to keep me on track and moving forward.

I am much indebted to Kevin Lippert of Princeton Architectural Press for inviting me to do this book. I am lucky to have a great editor, Linda Lee, who worked so graciously to guide my book through the publication process. Her comments on the manuscript were invaluable and helped me clarify the intent of my writing. Dorothy Ball, whom we now affectionately refer to as the surgeon general, did a remarkable job of reviewing the manuscript, ensuring the text is clear, and asking for the missing transitions that make navigation through text flow smoothly. I am also grateful to Deb Wood, the design director at PAP, who respectfully commented on our design and provided useful feedback along the way. Thanks also to their cohorts who worked behind the scenes to guide *The Wayfinding Handbook* from manuscript to printed books. And finally, thanks to Clare Jacobson, executive editor at PAP, who helped nurture the project in the early stages.

I am very grateful to the clients and professional colleagues who shared their insights and experience for the sidebar commentaries: Ann Harakawa, Craig M. Berger, Anthony Ferrara, Neil Kittredge, Sylvia Harris, Jonathan Hoefler, Leatrice Eiseman, Jack and Gay Reineck, Tomas J. Rossant, Rohit Aggarwala, Howard Landers, Sarah Haun, and Donall Healy. And a special thanks to Christopher Pullman, my professor from Yale School of Art and long-time friend who provided the book's delightful foreword. Craig M. Berger of the Society for Environmental Graphic Design generously shared ideas and resources to help fill out this book. Thanks also to my friends and colleagues in the design world who provided images and illustrations to help make the words come to life. I am grateful to those of my colleagues who have written about signage, wayfinding, and environmental graphics before me—their work is an inspiration, and they have helped to create a narrative of the profession and practice of wayfinding.

Finally, a special thanks to three people: my colleague and fellow Two Twelve principal Ann Harakawa for believing in this project, encouraging me, and giving me the time and space to undertake it; my dear friend Jonathan Ned Katz, who taught me to write by example and by years of his editorial advice; and to my domestic partner, Rich Kiamco, whose love and support keep me going each day.

BIBLIOGRAPHY

Environmental graphic design and wayfinding encompass many disciplines, as indicated by the range of subjects below. Many out-of-print texts, useful as inspiration and for reference, are available in design libraries or through specialty book dealers.

ARCHITECTURE AND PLANNING

Bacon, Edward M.
The Design of Cities.
New York: Viking Press, 1967.
Vivid, visual account of the historical development of the city.

Blake, Peter.
God's Own Junkyard: The Planned Deterioration of America's Landscape.
New York: Holt, Rinehart and Winston, 1964.
Prescient protest about the built environment's demise.

Crosby, Theo.
Architecture: City Sense.
New York: Studio Vista/ Reinhold, 1965.
Early appeal for enlightened city planning in artful book design.

Girouard, Mark.
Cities & People: A Social and Architectural History.
New Haven, CT: Yale University Press, 1985.
Lavishly illustrated history by a British historian.

Halprin, Lawrence.
Cities.
New York: Reinhold, 1963.
Presents urban spaces as works of art and living entities.

Jackson, John Brinckerhoff.
A Sense of Place, a Sense of Time.
New Haven, CT: Yale University Press, 1994.
Final reflections from a pioneering landscape architect.

Kunstler, James Howard.
The Geography of Nowhere: The Rise and Decline of America's Man-made Landscape.
New York: Simon & Schuster, 1993.
Readable rant that offers some solutions.

Lynch, Kevin.
The Image of the City.
Cambridge, MA: MIT Press, 1960.
Classic urban planning text that coined the term *way-finding.*

Mitchell, William J.
City of Bits: Space, Place and the Infobahn.
Cambridge, MA: MIT Press, 1996.
New cyber territories with parallels to real space.

Moholy-Nagy, Sibyl.
Matrix of Man: An Illustrated History of Urban Environment.
New York: Praeger, 1968.
Having "faith in the historical city."

Paumier, Cy.
Creating a Vibrant City Center.
Washington, DC: ULI—The Urban Land Institute, 2004.
How urban planning can revitalize downtown areas.

Pevsner, Nikolaus.
The Sources of Modern Architecture and Design.
Rev. ed. London: Thames & Hudson, 1968.
Great visual resource.

Rudofsky, Bernard.
Streets for People: A Primer for Americans.
New York: Doubleday, 1969.
A short visual history proves that streets can be designed as "oases rather than deserts."

Rybczynski, Witold.
City Life.
New York: Touchstone/Simon & Schuster, 1995.
Study on cities "as they are, not as they might be."

Scully, Vincent, Jr.
Modern Architecture.
Rev. ed. New York: George Braziller, 1994.
This edition of the 1961 classic covers urban planning.

Sudjic, Deyan.
The 100 Mile City.
San Diego: Harcourt Brace, 1992.
From industrial bases to information complexes.

Turner, Paul Venable.
Campus: An American Planning Tradition.
Cambridge, MA: MIT Press, 1984.
An essential guide to academic-facility planning.

Venturi, Robert.
Complexity and Contradiction in Architecture.
New York: Museum of Modern Art, 1977.
Update of the classic 1966 text by iconoclastic Pritzker-winning author of *Learning from Las Vegas.*

Whyte, William.
City: Rediscovering the Center.
New York: Doubleday, 1988.
Follows up the "City Spaces/ Human Places" episode of NOVA.

ENVIRONMENTAL GRAPHIC DESIGN, SIGNAGE, AND WAYFINDING

Arthur, Paul, and Romedi Passini.
Wayfinding: People, Signs, and Architecture.
New York: McGraw-Hill, 1992.
Arthur, a leader in the field, helped to build respect for wayfinding as a design profession.

Baines, Phil, and Catherine Dixon.
Signs, Lettering in the Environment.
London: Laurence King, 2003.
Carries on the research of Bartram, Gray, and others.

Ballinger, Raymond A.
Lettering Art in Modern Use.
New York: Reinhold, 1954.
Pictorial, presents many signing illustrations.

Bartram, Alan.
Lettering on Architecture.
New York: Whitney Library of Design, 1975.
Great visual reference for early British and Italian signs.

Berger, Craig M.
Wayfinding: Designing and Implementing Graphic Navigational Systems.
Mies, Switzerland: RotoVision, 2005.
Profession and industry overview compiled for the Society for Environmental Graphic Design (SEGD).

Calori, Chris.
Signage and Wayfinding Design: A Complete Guide to Creating Environmental Graphic Design Systems.
Hoboken, NJ: John Wiley & Sons, 2007.
Comprehensive teaching text by an EGD expert.

Carr, Stephen.
City Signs and Lights: A Policy Study Prepared for the Boston Redevelopment Authority and the U.S. Dept. of Housing & Urban Development.
Cambridge, MA: MIT Press, 1973.
In-depth study about improving urban travel conditions.

Cato, Ken, and Leigh Cato.
Graphics in the Third Dimension.
Tokyo: Graphic Sha, 1992.
Visual survey of signage and total-environment design.

Constantine, Mildred, and Egbert Jacobson.
Sign Language for Buildings and Landscape.
New York: Reinhold, 1961.
Seminal text about architectural graphics.

Crosby/Fletcher/Forbes.
A Sign Systems Manual.
New York: Praeger, 1970.
Early primer covering sign layout principles.

Finke, Gail Deibler.
City Signs: Innovative Urban Graphics.
New York: Madison Square Press, 1994.
Case studies of urban programs in the United States and Canada.

Follis, John, and Dave Hammer.
Architectural Signing and Graphics.
New York: Whitney Library of Design, 1979.
Primer by an EGD pioneer.

Fox, Martin, ed.
Print Casebooks. The Best in Environmental Graphics. Vols. 1–8.
Rockville, MD: RC Publications, 1975–91.
Inventory of case studies reflecting style changes.

Gallery-Dilworth, Leslie, ed., and Finke, Gail Diebler.
You Are Here: Graphics that Direct, Explain & Entertain.
Cincinnati: ST Publications, 1999.
Overview of award-winning projects from the SEGD.

Gray, Nicolete.
Lettering on Buildings.
London: Architectural Press, 1960.
Important, seminal research that influenced Bartram's research.

Herdeg, Walter, ed.
Archigraphia.
Zurich: Graphis Press, 1981.
Inspirational visual survey of international EGD projects.

Hunt, Wayne, ed.
Designing and Planning Environmental Graphics.
New York: Madison Square Press, 1995.
Case studies ranging from sign systems to entertainment environments.

Kinneir, Jock.
Words and Buildings: The Art of Public Lettering.
London: Architectural Press, 1980.
Excellent historic survey by a British expert.

Miller, J. Abbott.
Signs and Spaces.
New York: Rockport Allworth Editions, 1994.
Contemporary profiles of companies that specialize in EGD; thoughtful essays.

Mollerup, Per.
Wayshowing: A Guide to Environmental Signage, Principles and Practices.
Baden, Switzerland: Lars Müller, 2005.
A theoretical, idiosyncratic, and comprehensive primer.

Sutton, James.
Signs in Action.
London: Studio Vista, 1965.
Small, artful book about vernacular and early modern signing in cities and on highways.

Symbol Signs.
New York: American Institute of Graphic Arts, 1975.
Report for the U.S. Department of Transportation. Important research project presented a rationale and standard pictogram art based on worldwide symbol survey.

GRAPHIC DESIGN, COLOR, AND TYPOGRAPHY

Albers, Josef.
The Interaction of Color.
New Haven, CT: Yale University Press, 1975.
Visual phenomena through color combinations.

Drucker, Johanna and McVarish, Emily.
Graphic Design History: A Critical Guide.
New York: Pearson Prentice Hall, 2008.
Landmark graphic design work considered in social and historical contexts.

Eiseman, Leatrice.
Color: Messages and Meanings, A Pantone Color Resource.
Gloucester, MA: Hand Books Press, 2008.
An expert weighs in on color psychology and trends.

Fabre, Maurice.
A History of Communications. Vol. 9, The New Illustrated Library of Science and Invention.
New York: Hawthorn Books, 1963.
See esp. chap. 5, "Communications through Space."

Friedman, Mildred, ed.
Graphic Design in America: A Visual Language History.
Minneapolis: Walker Art Center; New York: Harry N. Abrams, 1989.
Catalog for a landmark exhibition at the IBM Gallery.

Frutiger, Adrian.
Type Sign Symbol.
Zurich: ABC Verlag, 1980.
A master designer explains his methodology.

Gray, Nicolete.
A History of Lettering: Creative Experiment and Letter Identity.
London: Phaidon, 1986.
Essential reference including many photos of dimensional examples.

Hollis, Richard.
Graphic Design: A Concise History.
London: Thames & Hudson, 1994.
Quick and readable reference that includes historic EGD examples.

Lupton, Ellen.
Thinking with Type: A Critical Guide for Designers, Writers, Editors, and Students.
New York: Princeton Architectural Press, 2004.
Authoritative primer by a master teacher, historian, and designer.

Macmillan, Neil.
An A–Z of Type Designers.
New Haven, CT: Yale University Press, 2006.
Beautiful sourcebook about type design from the Renaissance to the present.

Pflughaupt, Laurent.
Letter by Letter: An Alphabetical Miscellany.
New York: Princeton Architectural Press, 2008.
Nuanced analysis of the western alphabet, with an emphasis on the Roman letter.

Rand, Paul.
Design, Form, and Chaos.
New Haven, CT: Yale University Press, 1993.
Master designer and teacher explains what shapes good design.

Robinson, Andrew.
The Story of Writing: Alphabets, Hieroglyphs & Pictograms.
London: Thames & Hudson, 1995.
Readable, well-illustrated chronology of written language.

Spiekermann, Erik, and E. M. Ginger.
Stop Stealing Sheep and Find Out How Type Works.
Berkeley, CA: Adobe Press Book, 2003.
Witty, irreverent, and full of useful tips.

INFORMATION DESIGN AND MAPPING

Akerman, James R., and Robert W. Karrow Jr., eds.
Maps: Finding our Place in the World.
Chicago: University of Chicago Press, 2007.
How maps link to culture and history, heavily illustrated.

Makower, Joel, ed.
The Map Catalog.
New York: Vintage Books/Random House, 1992.
Annotated list of map types and software.

Ovenden, Mark.
Transit Maps of the World: The World's First Collection of Every Urban Train Map on Earth.
London: Penguin, 2007.
Amazing visual compendium.

Southworth, Michael, and Susan Southworth.
Maps: A Visual Survey and Design Guide.
Boston: A New York Graphic Society Book by Little, Brown and Company, 1982.
Historic examples of the many forms maps take.

Tufte, Edward R.
Beautiful Evidence.
Cheshire, CT: Graphics Press, 2006.
The fourth in a quintet of fascinating texts about information display.

Wildbur, Peter, and Michael Burke.
Information Graphics: Innovative Solutions to Contemporary Design.
New York: Thames & Hudson, 1998.
Visual survey of information design in all media.

Wurman, Richard Saul.
Information Architects.
New York: Graphis, 1996.
Defines information design as a unique, essential specialization.

——.
"Making the City Observable."
Special issue, Design Quarterly 80 (1971).
Boldly graphic visualization of cityscapes.

PRODUCT DESIGN, MATERIALS, AND TECHNOLOGY

Aczel, Amir D.
The Riddle of the Compass: The Invention that Changed the World.
New York: Harcourt, 2001.
Tracks the history of the wayfinder's ultimate tool.

Antonelli, Paola, ed.
Design and the Elastic Mind.
New York: Museum of Modern Art, 2008.
Landmark exhibition catalog presenting innovative responses to accelerated social, technological, and scientific change.

Bell, Victoria Ballard, and Patrick Rand.
Materials for Design.
New York: Princeton Architectural Press, 2006.
Useful guide that bridges the gap between construction materials and design sensibility.

Brownell, Blaine.
Transmaterial 1+2: A Catalog of Materials that Redefine our Physical Environment.
New York: Princeton Architectural Press, 2008.
Comprehensive reference in two volumes by popular "Product of the Week" website author.

Dreyfuss, Henry.
Designing for People.
New York: Viking Press, 1974.
Classic text first published in 1955 with foreword by R. Buckminster Fuller.

Hoke, John Ray, Jr.
Ramsey/Sleeper, Architectural Graphic Standards.
New York: John Wiley & Sons, 2000.
The classic text on architectural detailing.

Norman, Donald A.
The Psychology of Everyday Things.
New York: Basic Books, 1988.
Best seller about why some products satisfy and others frustrate consumers.

——.
Emotional Design: Why We Love (or Hate) Everyday Things.
New York: Basic Books, 2004.
Argues that good products are not merely functional, but attractive and fun to use.

RESOURCES

UNIVERSAL AND SUSTAINABLE DESIGN

Benyus, Janine M.
Biomimicry: Innovation Inspired by Nature.
New York: HarperCollins, 1997.
Intriguing discussion of the parallels between design concepts and natural systems.

Carpman, Janet R., and Myron A. Grant.
Design That Cares: Planning Health Facilities for Patients and Visitors.
2nd ed. San Francisco: Jossey-Bass, 2001.
Practical, illustrated primer on design for the disabled.

McDonough, William, and Michael Braungart.
Cradle to Cradle: Remaking the Way We Make Things.
New York: North Point Press, 2002.
Provocative theories about product life cycles by pioneering architect and visionary chemist.

Papanek, Victor.
Design for the Real World: Human Ecology and Social Change.
New York: Pantheon Books, 1971.
Impassioned early argument for responsible design.

PROFESSIONAL ASSOCIATIONS

The American Institute of Architects (AIA)
1735 New York Ave., NW
Washington, DC 20006-5292
800.AIA.3837 (800.242.3837)
202.626.7300
www.aia.org

AIGA
164 Fifth Ave.
New York, NY 10010
212.807.1990
www.aiga.org

American Planning Association (APA)
1776 Massachusetts Ave., NW
Suite 400
Washington, DC 20036-1904
202.872.0611
www.planning.org

American Society of Interior Designers (ASID)
608 Massachusetts Ave., NE
Washington, DC 20002-6006
202.546.3480
www.asid.org

American Society of Landscape Architects (ASLA)
636 Eye St., NW
Washington, DC 20001-3736
888.999.ASLA (888.999.2752)
202.898.2444
www.asla.org

Association for Computing Machinery Special Interest Group on Computer Graphics and Interactive Techniques (ACM Siggraph)
www.siggraph.org

Association of Professional Design Firms (APDF)
1448 East 52nd St., #201
Chicago, IL 60615
773.643.7052
www.apdf.org

Building Owners and Managers Association (BOMA)
1101 15th St., NW
Suite 800
Washington, DC 20005
202.408.2662
www.boma.org

Center for Design and Business
Rhode Island School of Design
169 Weybosset St.
Providence, RI 02902
401.454.6558
www.centerdesignbusiness.org

Corporate Design Foundation
20 Park Plaza
Suite 400
Boston, MA 02116-4303
617.566.7676
www.cdf.org

Design Council
34 Bow St.
London WC2E 7DL
United Kingdom
+44.(0)20.7420.5200
www.designcouncil.org.uk

Design Management Institute
101 Tremont St.
Suite 300
Boston, MA 02108
617.338.6380
www.dmi.org

Institute of Transportation Engineers (ITE)
1099 14th St., NW
Suite 300 West
Washington, DC 20005-3438
202.289.0222
www.ite.org

The International Association of Lighting Designers (IALD)
The Merchandise Mart
Suite 9-104
Chicago, IL 60654
312.527.3677
www.iald.org

The International Code Council (ICC)
500 New Jersey Ave., NW
6th Floor
Washington, DC 20001-2070
888.ICC.SAFE (888.422.7233)
www.iccsafe.org

International Council of Graphic Design Associations (Icograda)
455 Saint Antoine Ouest
Suite SS 10
Montréal, Québec
Canada H2Z 1J1
+1.514.448.4949 x 221
www.icograda.org

Industrial Designers Society of America (IDSA)
45195 Business Court
Suite 250
Dulles, VA 20166-6717
703.707.6000
www.idsa.org

International Facility Management Association (IFMA)
1 E. Greenway Plaza
Suite 1100
Houston, TX 77046-0194
713.623.4362
www.ifma.org

The International Institute for Information Design (IIID)
Palffygasse 27/16
1170, Vienna
Austria
+43.(0)1.403.66.62
www.iiid.net

International Interior Design
Association (IIDA)
222 Merchandise Mart Plaza
Suite 567
Chicago, IL 60654-1103
888.799.IIDA (888.799.4432)
www.iida.org

International Sign Association
(ISA)
1001 N. Fairfax St.
Suite 301
Alexandria, VA 22314
703.836.4012
www.signs.org

The Sign Design Society (SDS)
5 Longton Grove, Sydenham
London
SE26 6QQ United Kingdom
+44.20.8776.8866
www.signdesignsociety.co.uk

Society for College and
University Planning (SCUP)
339 E. Liberty
Suite 300
Ann Arbor, MI 48104
734.998.7832
www.scup.org

Society for Environmental
Graphic Design (SEGD)
1000 Vermont Ave., NW,
Suite 400
Washington, DC 20005
202.638.5555
www.segd.org

Society for Marketing
Professional Services (SMPS)
44 Canal Center Plaza
Suite 444
Alexandria, VA 22314
800.292.7677
703.549.6117
www.smps.org

Urban Land Institute (ULI)
1025 Thomas Jefferson St., NW
Suite 500 West
Washington, DC 20007
202.624.7000
www.uli.org

GREEN RESOURCES

Forest Stewardship Council
(FSC)
11100 Wildlife Center Dr.
Suite 100
Reston, VA 20190
703.438.6401
www.fscus.org

Global Green USA Headquarters
2218 Main St.
2nd Floor
Santa Monica, CA 90405
310.581.2700
www.globalgreen.org

Green Seal
1001 Connecticut Ave., NW
Suite 827
Washington, D.C. 20036-5525
202.872.6400
202.872.4324
www.greenseal.org

Rainforest Alliance
665 Broadway
Suite 500
New York, NY 10012
212.677.1900
888.MY-EARTH (888-693-2784)
www.rainforest-alliance.org

United States Environmental
Protection Agency (EPA)
Ariel Rios Building
1200 Pennsylvania Ave., NW
Washington, DC 20460
202.272.0167
www.epa.gov

U.S. Green Building Council
1800 Massachusetts Ave., NW
Suite 300
Washington, DC 20036
800.795.1747
202.742.3792
www.usgbc.org

MATERIALS, DESIGN, AND
TECHNICAL RESOURCES

The Center for Health Design
1850 Gateway Blvd.
Suite 1083
Concord, CA 94520
925.521.9404
www.healthdesign.org

Eiseman Center for Color
Information and Training
www.colorexpert.com

Glass Association of
North America
2945 SW Wanamaker Dr.
Suite A
Topeka, KS 66614-5321
785.271.0208
www.glasswebsite.com

International Organization
for Standardization (ISO)
1, ch. de la Voie-Creuse
Case postale 56
CH-1211 Geneva 20
Switzerland
+41.22.749.02.22
www.standardsinfo.net

Manual of Uniform Traffic
Control Devices (MUTCD)
Office of Transportation
Operations (HOTO)
Federal Highway Administration,
Mail Stop: E84-402
1200 New Jersey Ave., SE
Washington, DC 20590
www.mutcd.fhwa.dot.gov

Material ConneXion
127 West 25th St.
2nd Floor
New York, NY 10001
212.842.2050
www.materialconnexion.com

MatWeb
Searchable Database of
Material Properties
2020 Kraft Dr.
Suite 3000
Blacksburg, VA 24060
540.552.5300
www.matweb.com

Mijksenaar Foundation,
Archives and Library
Amstelveste
Joan Muyskenweg 22
1096 CJ Amsterdam
The Netherlands
+31.(0)20.691.47.29
www.mijksenaar.com

National Association for
Surface Finishing (NASF)
1155 Fifteenth St., NW
Suite 500
Washington, DC 20005
202.457.8404
www.nasf.org

National Metal Finishing
Resource Center
734.995.4911
www.nmfrc.org

Pantone, Inc.
World Headquarters
590 Commerce Blvd.
Carlstadt, NJ 07072-3098
201.935.5500
www.pantone.com

Stone Source
215 Park Ave. South
New York, NY 10003
212.979.6400
www.stonesource.com

IMAGE CREDITS

All drawings © Two Twelve Associates unless otherwise noted.

4–5 Ken Yuel. 10–11 Jamie Fake. 12 Karl Grupe/Getty Images (L). Martin Puddy/Getty Images (ML). Karan Kapoor/Getty Images (MR). David Gibson (R). 13 David Gibson (L, ML). James Balog/Getty Images (MR). Greg Pease/Getty Images (R). 14 Nick Spriggs (L). David Gibson (ML–R). 15 Marissa Edwards (L). David Gibson (ML, MR). Nick Spriggs (R). 16 Julie Park (L). David Gibson (M, R). 17 Jim Simmons/Corbin Design, Hunt Design and Urban Place Consulting Group: Downtown LA Walks (T). Shinichi Tonita/REI Design & Plannings: Toyko Big Sight (MR). J. Miles Wolf/Sussman/Prejza & Company: Duke Energy Center (ML). Peter Mauss/Esto/Pentagram: Salt Lake City Public Library (B). 20 Two Twelve: Princeton University (TL). Vignelli Associates: The Museum of Fine Arts, Houston (TR). Gottschalk + Ash International: Ottawa International Airport (ML). YoungDoo Moon (MR). David Sunberg/Esto/Pentagram: Arizona Cardinals Stadium (BL). Jim Simmons/Sussman/Prejza & Company: Universal CityWalk (BM). Two Twelve: 731 Lexington Avenue (BR). 21 HLW International: Rallye BMW (TL). Hedrich Blessing Photography/Gensler: Wilson Sporting Goods (TR). emerystudio Australia: Manchester Civil Justice Centre (ML). Two Twelve: Grand Central Market (M); Massachusetts General Hospital (MR); Hartford Streetscape (BL); Sound Tranist (BR). 22 Vignelli Associates: 712 Fifth Avenue (TL). Lucy Liow (TR). Jonathan H. Posnett (BL). Two Twelve: Rockefeller Center (BM). Poulin + Morris: Penn South (BR). 23 Meeker & Associates: Clearview Highway Signage (T). Lorenc + Yoo Design: NC State University (ML).

Dion Bruins (MR). Two Twelve: Scenic Hudson (BL); Times Square Tower (BR). Angelica Solis/Newsom Design: North Market (BM). 24 Julie Park. 25, 26 Greg Kinch. 29 Craig M. Berger. 30–31 Spencer Cheng. 32 Jonathan H. Posnett. 36 Wally Gobetz (L). Jonathan H. Posnett (R). 37 Jonathan H. Posnett. 38 Digital Globe (TR). Jason Hawkes (BL). Thomas H. Williams (BR). 40 London Transit Museum. 44 Joel Katz Design Associates: Walk!Philadelphia. 45 Roll Barresi & Associates: Brigham and Women's Hospital. 46 (L–R) Vignelli Associates: International Design Center of New York. Nick Spriggs. Anton Grassl/Selbert Perkins Design: Pacific Design Center. Roll Barresi & Associates: City of Newport. Hadakogeisha: Nakagawamachi-kira Junior High School. Gottschalk + Ash International: Boston Convention Center. Jim Simmons/Sussman/ Prejza & Company: Van Nuys FlyAway. 47 Design Mijksenaar, Amsterdam and Mijksenaar ARUP Wayfinding, New York: Amsterdam Airport Schiphol. 48 Don F. Wong/Pentagram: Minnesota Children's Museum (T). David Gibson (L). Anton Grassl/Selbert Perkins Design: LAX Airport (M). Bruce Mau Design: Walt Disney Concert Hall (B). 49 Poulin + Morris: Heimbold Visual Arts Center (TL). emerystudio Australia: City Museum (TM). The Office of Michael Manwaring: HP Pavilion at San Jose (TR). Punchstock (BL). Nigel Swales (BR). 50 Catherine Dixon (T). Julie Park (L). emerystudio Australia: Melbourne Docklands (B). 51 Christopher A. Tarantino (TL). emerystudio Australia: Eureka Carpark (TR). MetaDesign AG: Düsseldorf International Airport (BL). Two Twelve: Shea Stadium (BR). 52 Kramer Design

Associates: INFOTOGO (T). Gottschalk + Ash International: Ottawa International Airport (B). 53 Meeker & Associates: The National Park Sevice Uniguide Program (TL). Warren S. Taylor (TR). Christopher A. Tarantino (ML). Nacâsa & Partners/Kotobuki Corporation: Pacifico Yokohama Exhibition Hall (MR). Chris Cooper Photography/Cloud Gehshan Associates: University of Texas (BR). 54 Matthew Yu (T). Two Twelve: Chicago Park District (L); Yale University (MR). Total Identity: IJburg Diemerpark (B). 55 Andrew Tomlinson (TL). Christopher A. Tarantino (TR). Two Twelve: Queens West Development Corporation Parks (BL); No Smoking (BR). 56 Two Twelve: American Airlines Center. 62 Two Twelve: Children's Hospital Boston. 63 Two Twelve: MoMA QNS. 64 Two Twelve: Massachusetts General Hospital (T, B). 66–67 Peter Specht. 69 Cindy Seigle (T). Jonathan H. Posnett (L). Darrell Harden (B). 70 Jonathan H. Posnett. 71 Michael A. Oakes (BR). 72 Two Twelve: Yale University (L). 73 Lou Ann M. Aepelbacher. 74 Carbone Smolan Agency: Talleyrand Office Park (T). Peter Mauss/Esto/ Pentagram: New Jersey Performing Arts Center (M). Juriaan Simonis (B). 75 Claire Bamford (T). Catherine Dixon (M). 76 New York Historical Society (T). Two Twelve: Radio City Music Hall (BL); Sound Transit (BR). 78 Dr. Antonio Comia (TL). Poulin + Morris: Holland Performing Arts Center (TM). Jeffrey Norman (TR). Two Twelve: West Midtown Ferry Terminal (BL). Peter Mauss/Esto/ Pentagram: Children's Museum of Pittsburgh (BM). Gottschalk + Ash International: Ottawa International Airport (BR). 86 Lindsay Flinn. 87 Kevin Schafer/Getty Images (L). Jade Berman (R). 89 Designgruppe Flath & Frank: Cologne/Bonn

Airport. 90 Kurt Paris (L). Anna Szabo (R). 91 Aioi Pro Photo/Maya Nakamuta: San-Ai Clinic (T). Beck & Graboski Design Office: Santa Monica Civic Center Parking Structure (M). Two Twelve: Children's Hospital Boston (BL); Radio City Music Hall (BM). Darlene Levy (BR). 92 Design Mijksenaar, Amsterdam and Mijksenaar ARUP Wayfinding, New York: JFK International Airport (T); Newark Liberty International Airport (B). 93 Two Twelve: Downtown Baltimore (T). Frost Design: Darling Harbour, Sydney Signage (B). 94 Peter Mauss/Esto/Pentagram: Wave Hill (T, B). Jonathan H. Posnett (L). 96 Hadakogeisha: Nakagawamachi-kira Junior High School (T). Punchstock (B). 97 Adler & Schmidt Kommunications-Design GmbH, Berlin: Rheinland-Pflaz (BL). 99 Otl Aicher: Munich 1972 (TL). Landor: Atlanta 1996 (TML). R-co: Sydney 2000 (TMR). China Central Academy of Fine Arts/Academy of Arts and Design: Beijing 2008 (TR). Citigate Lloud Northover (M). Aichi Perfectural University of Fine Arts and Music/GK Design Group: Limino Stations (B). 106 Matthew Cohen. 107 Anton Grassl/Selbert Perkins Design: Mount Holyoke College (T). Joel Katz Design Associates: MIT (M). NPK Design: Floriade Haarlemmermeer (B). 108 Two Twelve: Beacon Court (T); Children's Hospital Boston (ML); Atlanta Federal Center (MR); KeySpan Park (B). 113 Jim Baxter. 118 Poulin + Morris: WGBH (L). Ingrid Chou (R). 119 Potion: National World War One Museum (T). Jonathan H. Posnett (B). 124 Two Twelve: Scenic Hudson (T); Northern Arizona University (B). 126–27 Eric Firley. 131 Two Twelve: City of Charlotte.

T (Top), M (Middle), B (Bottom), L (Left), R (Right)

INDEX